Karen —
The gift of this book is an invit-
to think beyond the book —
not a request to agree with the auth.
Ed DeJean

A Belief System from Beyond the Box

Edgar K. DeJean

authorHOUSE®

AuthorHouse™
1663 Liberty Drive, Suite 200
Bloomington, IN 47403
www.authorhouse.com
Phone: 1-800-839-8640

First published by AuthorHouse 4/24/2009

ISBN: 978-1-4389-6788-2 (sc)
ISBN: 978-1-4389-6787-5 (hc)

Printed in the United States of America
Bloomington, Indiana

This book is printed on acid-free paper.

Preface

*"You got to be very careful if you don't know where
you're going, because you might not get there."*
Yogi Berra

On Friday, May 27, 2005 I am starting something. I am told it is a blog. [Per Wikipedia Encyclopedia - A blog (an abridgment of the term web log) is a website, usually maintained by an individual, with regular entries of commentary, descriptions of events, or other material such as graphics or video. Entries are commonly displayed in reverse chronological order. "Blog" can also be used as a verb, meaning to maintain or add content to a blog.]

I have a limited understanding of what a blog is, but I am starting one. I have no idea of where my blog is taking me, but I am headed there. I use Yogi Berra's advice (see above) because I do comprehend the value of being careful: being careful where you go, being careful what you say, being careful where you leave what you say. In the case of a blog one leaves ones words floating in cyberspace available to anyone with a web browser. (Per Wikipedia Encyclopedia - "A web browser is a software application which enables a user to display and interact with text, images, videos, music and other information typically located on a Web page at a website on the World Wide Web or a local area network.)

v

Earlier in 2005 I had put my long-standing concerns about my personal belief system and my developing concerns about the future of the church into a small book, "A Belief System from the General Store."

My primary objective in starting a blog is to establish a meeting place where those who stumble onto my book can give me feed back on its content. I shall only infrequently quote participants directly but I shall use their comments to assist in an intelligible flow of blogs.

It is my hope that my long standing concerns about my personal belief system, and my expanding concerns about the direction of the church, can be vicarious incentives to my peers, inside and outside the church, as they think upon these personal and communal matters.

I do not purport to be a theologian nor an authority on church polity. I do claim the right to develop my personal belief system and to explore how the belief systems of all its members, and non-members, relate to the future of the church.

Although I cannot tell readers where we are going they will note that the title of the first blog is – "It's Beyond Me." . . . So here we go – "very carefully."

How to Convert a Blog to a Book.

Since the reader is reading this material from a book it is obvious that this blog series has been converted to - hard copy - as they say in the media world. The software used to publish material as blogs normally presents several deficits of format, font and punctuation. In traditional print systems these deficits can be corrected and herein we have attempted to do so.

At a given point I made the decision to publish these blogged thoughts. The reader will note that my style changed with that decision. In the beginning I was addressing the specific problems of the denomination where my belief system has been on deposit for 72 years. As I have come in contact with a broader base of peers from other denominations it is obvious that the concerns I am addressing are similar to theirs and vary only in specifics throughout the Christian faith.

My experiences within faiths other than Christian are limited but it is more and more obvious to me that all monotheistic religions diminish their Deity in their attempt to render that God anthropomorphic and comprehensible and their written descriptions inerrant and infallible.

Early in the blogs the reader may begin to lose interest with all the references to the Presbyterian Church in the United States of America (PCUSA) - especially if the readers are of another faith. Do not lose heart. I believe there are many valid, generic, ecumenical truths in those early blogs before the author transposes to the basic, generic problem, "The Christian Church must change or it will die."

Lest that statement be a too harsh realization, the author comes later to a softer recognition of the future – "The Church must morph to survive."

An afterthought:

Sometimes I am tempted to read the conclusions of nonfiction (not fiction) books to see if I want to read the rest of the book. Here I would **encourage** the reader to read the final blog of the series:

Friday, December 12, 2008

TFTU 20. And Now – In Conclusion

Then read the Epilogue **plus** About the Author.

Thereafter I hope that readers will read in normal sequence to discover how response-able persons can think beyond the box (containing the ABCs of the Comprehensible God of the Bible Verse) into the unlimited expanses of the **Incomprehensible God of the Universe.**

Friday May 27, 2005

It's Beyond Me

Recently I was in conversation with a man who had just read "A Belief System from the General Store." He told me that he had enjoyed the anecdotal stories about my youth. He told me further that he is searching very seriously for a pragmatic belief system.

I told him that I share in that search. I hinted that I hoped the book contained some do-it-yourself ideas that might help his search. As our conversation moved from the routines of living to the beliefs of life, he was willing to go a certain distance. But, when we left what he considered the pragmatic and tiptoed into what he felt to be spiritual he voiced his discomfort as, "It's beyond me."

Of course the spiritual is "beyond" us. But it is also "with us, within us, joining us together." Why have we permitted the routines of living (reality) to become separated from the beliefs of existence (the spiritual)? Why have we permitted religions to usurp the spiritual and define what they infer remains - using the term secular? Why have we not only permitted but encouraged perceptions and stories from previous cultures to become the book religions which shape our belief systems although we live within today's vastly different cultures with rapidly expanding knowledge bases?

Much has changed in our knowledge of the universe since the human emerged beyond instinctual action to the capability of intellectual choice. Our early ancestors chose to relate to the spiritual as God and ascribed to that God a Spiritual Kingdom that differs from earthly kingdoms. Over the ages as the spiritual and societal worths of the individual have evolved, human relationships have also become more valued and far better understood. We still have ages to go but there is a growing intellectual/spiritual awareness around the world that the entire human family is eventually intended to relate through a **Kindom** with other humans under God as opposed to kingdoms of humans under kings.

My belief system tells me it will happen. My reality systems have no idea how many eons it will take.

Tuesday, May 31, 2005

Christianity

How can anyone say that Christianity doesn't work when no one has ever tried it? (Mark Twain)

Thursday June 2, 2005

June 2, 2005
Christianity Practiced

People are equally horrified at hearing the Christian religion doubted, and at seeing it practiced. (Samuel Butler)

Monday, June 20, 2005

Why Bother?

Someone who had not yet read "A Belief System from the General Store" asked me, "Why did you bother to write a book which very few people will read?"

This was not a disparaging remark from a negative person. It was a consoling query from an empathetic friend. No one had asked me this question and it gave me pause. That pause resulted in this answer, "I've finally lived long enough that I have discovered something I want to say, and more people may hear it if it's in a book than if it's sealed up with me and my best suit in a concrete vault."

What is this that I want to say? Do I need to unload a lifetime of heavy conscience? "No." Have I learned something worth passing on? "I think so."

I have discovered that there are two kinds of people who can't define God. There are those who try to and those who don't try to. Too often it is those religious folks who try the hardest who dust up the most misery for others, no doubt including God.

I have also discovered two imperative questions.

1. Does Christianity need to change its manner of teaching so that its adherents can be more response-able to God?

2. Can it effect these changes?

My answer to Number 1 is, "Yes." My answer to Number 2 is, "I hope so."

Monday, June 27, 2005

It Is Monday

It Is Monday.

After yesterday's day of rest I assume that we of the Presbyterian Church United States of America (PCUSA) can return to our factional claims that our group knows and shows best the Will of God and thus is justified in our mistrust of those of our Presbyterian Communion with whom we are in impasse.

If the reader of this blog is a Presbyterian - What can we do?

If the reader is not a Presbyterian - Your ideas may be even more objective!

Two quotes from Edwin Markham as starters:

He drew a circle that shut me out.
Heretic, rebel, a thing to flout.
But love and I had the wit to win;
We drew a circle that took him in.
(Outwitted)

We have committed the Golden Rule to memory;
Let us now commit it to life.

Monday, July 4, 2005

Independence Day for the United States

July 4, 2005 is very different from July 4, 1776.

In 1776 there were tsunamis, earthquakes, hurricanes, tornados, floods, volcanic eruptions, wars, disease, slavery, man's inhumanities to man.....

In this day there are tsunamis, earthquakes, hurricanes, tornados, floods, volcanic eruptions, wars, disease, slavery, man's inhumanities to man ... AND

depletion of resources, greenhouse gases, global warming, toxic wastes, potential for nuclear winter ... any one of these can/would be fatal to human life on this planet, and all can be traced directly to the presence of the human on the planet.

Let's start now to work toward an Interdependence Day for all the World's States!

Sunday July 10, 2005

Meditation

It is Sunday which thus far has been - an early breakfast out with friends, the newspaper, worship with more friends, a nap at home, a sandwich out.

Pastor Sara rated this morning's pulpit presentation a "Meditation," which the dictionary defines as: noun • the action or practice of meditating • a written or spoken discourse expressing considered thought on a subject.

Sara's title was: "Everything, Finally, is Grace."

Her spoken discourse was convincingly accurate and her conclusion was the challenge for hearers to continue their meditating on her meditation.

I am. The result I need most is: "How to be, finally, Grace full."

Monday, July 25, 2005

What's A Blog?

When one logs onto ones web site and leaves an entry on the log this has come to be known as a "blog." All this started as recently in internet happenings as 1999. First the name "WeeLog" was used for such an entry. Gradually this was modified to "Web log" and finally became "blog."

Here is a concise definition of the word from a Google search:

"A frequent, chronological publication of personal thoughts and Web links. A blog is often a mixture of what is happening in a person's life and what is happening on the Web, a kind of hybrid diary/guide site, although there are as many unique types of blogs as there are people."

From NetLingo The Internet Dictionary

Here is a 1-2-3 way to learn more than you ever wanted to know about blogs and blogging -

Go to - www.netlingo.com
Click on the letter B in the index of letters
Scroll down to blog
In this window scroll down to "more info"
Use the 10 points there as your launching pad to the world of blogging.

Tuesday, August 2, 2005

Standing Before God

Pastor Sara's homily July 30 was titled, "Loving God with Heart and Mind. "It was based on Romans 14:1-13 and its homiletic point was Paul's explanation that we can hold differing beliefs at varying levels and still you -- and still I -- ALL OF US, can be response-able to God.

Sara's message was delivered at such a level of the consciousness of God that the thought came to me within its few minutes, "If every member of each congregation in the Presbyterian Church, U.S.A. were hearing this homily openly and searchingly, this denomination could find its way out of its current morass."

Friends, some of our Presbyterian brothers and sisters tell us that, because we do not believe what they believe, this makes us apostate and we are creating an impasse. I reject out of hand the label, apostate, and I would question who is doing the creating. Further -- what is created is not an impasse, it is a morass. Here I pause. There is a much more genteel synonym for morass.

It is imbroglio - noun - an extremely confused, complicated or embarrassing situation. -- We Presbyterians are in an imbroglio.

All we Presbyterians should be extremely embarrassed.

Here is Sara's answer to what I term imbroglio - a paragraph lifted word for word from her homily.

"How can we claim to draw near to the mind of God when, for whatever reasons, we will not draw near to the minds of each other? How can we attempt to understand the heart of the divine if we will not try to understand the hearts within ourselves and each other? How can we truly accept the strange and beautiful in reality if we cannot accept the strange and beautiful neighbors behind, before and beside us in these pews?"

Sara's homiletic, concluding paraphrase of Paul's words to the Romans: "We all stand before God, and God is able to make us stand."

And here I conclude this blog: "Therefore, let all of us cease our standing before God in a morass of imbroglio."

Tuesday, August 30, 2005

"The Layman" vs. We Laymen?

The Presbyterian Lay Committee is an organization that had its roots in the United Presbyterian Church in the U.S.A. in 1965.

Church History.

At the time of the Civil War the Presbyterian Church split into the "Northern" Church, the Presbyterian Church in the U.S.A. and the "Southern" Church, the Presbyterian Church in the U.S. In 1958 the Presbyterian Church in the U.S.A. came into a union with the United Presbyterian Church of North America to form the United Presbyterian Church in the U.S.A. Today's Presbyterian Church (U.S.A.) was formed in 1983 by the historic reunion of the "Northern" Church, The United Presbyterian Church in the U.S.A., and the "Southern" Church, the Presbyterian Church in the U.S.

Committee History

The Presbyterian Lay Committee publishes a newspaper: "The Layman."

The Committee's Mission Statement: The Mission of the Presbyterian Lay Committee is to inform and equip God's people by proclaiming Jesus Christ alone as:

- The Way of Salvation
- The Truth of God's Word.
- The Life of discipleship.

In its Newspaper beneath its Mission Statement it lists Five Objectives.

1. Emphasis on teaching the Bible.
2. Emphasize Jesus Christ as Lord and Savior.
3. Encourage individual Presbyterians to be involved in community.

4. Encourage church bodies to seek and express the mind of God.

5. To be a source of information on issues confronting the church.

Gradually - over its 40 years - its voice has become more strident and its faith system less flexible until it is now a faith within a faith. It is in a more or less adversarial relationship with the mother church and is currently asking the power laden question:

Can Two Faiths Embrace One Future?

The Lay Commitee claims impasse with those outside its faith designs and labels anyone who disagrees with its tenets apostate. In response to the Lay Committee's position I have written and mailed a letter to the Layman Editor which will not get published in The Layman, so I'll go ahead and publish it here .

To The Editor:

Could the fact that I have been a Presbyterian Lay Person longer than The Layman has been a publication give me a Grandfather status and permit me the temerity to ask a question in response to the Lay Committee's question: "Can two faiths embrace one future?"

Has God franchised the Lay Committee and The Layman to define, delimit and disown my faith, which falls in the second category, the one they define as apostate? Does God depend upon briefings on the future from The Layman's editorial board?

At first I was quite upset when The Layman told me I was apostate. Then God whispered in my ear, "Be calm, little man. You have a lot more to worry about than how The Layman describes you."

Ed DeJean
Salem, IN
posted by Ed DeJean | 2:21 PM

P.S. Amazingly - The letter was published on the Layman's Website.

Tuesday, September 6, 2005

Flippant or Faithful?

In last week's blog (August 30, 2005) I portrayed God as whispering in my ear.

Was I being anthropomorphically flippant or theistically faithful?

Anthropomorphic - means I define God as having super human-like characteristics through which I see God acting in human fashions e.g. God hears my "words" and "whispers" back to me.

Theistic - Although I do not attempt to define, describe or delimit God I attribute to the human theistic abilities to be response-able (faithful) to God. To give this relationship greater depth and authenticity we, as Christians, insert Christ as an intermediary e.g. "What a friend we have in Jesus."

We also try to authenticate our "personal" relationship with God by the insertion of other-world beings -- angels etc.

Once in a saintly passion
I cried with desperate grief,
Oh Lord, my heart is black with guile,
Of sinners I am chief.
Then stooped my guardian angel
And whispered from behind,
Vanity my little man,
You're nothing of the kind.

James Thompson

When others' concepts, tenets, doctrines of God and the (anthropomorphic) Mind of God differ from ours does this make theirs correct and ours wrong -- and thus they can declare us apostate?

An Ode to the Presbyterian Lay Committee

To the Lay
Com--mit--tee-
Oh the waste
Of en--er--gee,
When we dis--a--gree,
You and meeee.
(by - E...K...D)

Edgar K. DeJean

Monday, September 12, 2005

Come Home to Love

Last week I promised to continue the blog concerning my exchanges with The Layman. I learned on Wednesday that my letter to The Layman had been answered (warmly?) by another Layman reader. Here is that answer:

'Come home to orthodoxy. We're waiting to welcome you.'
August 29, 2005
I was reading with interest the letter you posted from Mr. Ed DeJean [August 26, 2005] taking you to task for having the temerity to describe the Bible-denying, Christ-disgracing, heresy-spewing, sodomy-embracing, baby-killing, new-age-spouting, synchronistic liberal faction in the PCUSA as "apostate." He seemed to be reveling in his self-identification as part of this category. How sad.

But I have cause for hope that Mr. DeJean may yet respond with repentance. The last sentence of Mr. DeJean's letter tells us of the warning he believes the God of the Bible whispered into his ear. For indeed, when you are apostate, "you have a lot more to worry about than how The Layman describes you."

May Mr. DeJean and all the heretics, apostates and unregenerate pagans who are part of the PCUSA corner of the visible church turn to Christ and find not only salvation for their souls but renewal of their minds, that they may demonstrate what is the good and acceptable and perfect will of God through the life-transforming power of the Holy Spirit.

Mr. DeJean, God has graciously given you a warning. Don't waste the opportunity. Come home to orthodoxy. We're waiting to welcome you.

Rev. Bill Pawson
Westminster Community Church
Canton, Ohio

I shared the above response with our Presbyterian (PCUSA) Brown Bag group at last Wednesday's gathering. They were shocked to learn about the real me (us). I promised to share my answer to Rev. Pawson at this Wednesday's (September 14, 2005) gathering. Here it is:

Come Home to Love
September 12, 2005

To the Editor and to my newly found friend, Rev. Bill Pawson:
(See Bill's letter to me, "Come home to orthodoxy. We're waiting to welcome you." August 29, 2005.)

Bill, I try really hard to make my home within an orthodoxy which reflects God's Grace. May God's Grace bring you home to Love.

Edgar DeJean, Elder
Salem, Indiana

Tuesday, September 20, 2005

Theistic Christians and (not vs.) Secular Christians

Recently our Pastor gave a benediction following morning worship in which she asked for God's blessings on Theistic Christians and on Secular Christians. I concur with the usage of the two terms.

I capitalize both adjectives, Theistic and Secular, because I believe that, in this usage, they are parts of two proper names. I believe that these two states of being do indeed exist and both are a part of the being or consciousness or intention of whatever is The Theistic Force. (God is the name often used.) I believe further that any separations between the two are the result of human errancies that can be corrected.

The human has been errant in pronouncing that the world is flat, declaring that the sun rotates around the earth; even stating that a Biblical character could manipulate God into making that sun stand still. In the past such statements have come from a lack of knowledge plus the misapplication of myth and hence could be termed innocent. Unfortunately the availability of more knowledge has not made the human less errant. Even as the opportunity for greater awareness comes to us, we cling all the more tenaciously to a growing list of erroneous errancies:

- The Earth's climate can withstand all human abuses.
- The Earth's resources are limitless.
- But - Fear not. Ruin the Earth. Move to Mars.
- Human poverty "will always be with us."
- Not all humans are Children of God in God's Kindom .
- Though not all folks are orthodox, thank God we are.

I am currently reading Karen Armstrong's book Battle for God. When she analyzes divisiveness within religions over the ages she uses the words mythos and logos as describing or explaining the stories of Christianity, for example. Mythos defines the story line of the spiritual or wished for and logos defines the story line of the historical or accepted. However, the comparative translations of theistic as mythos and secular as logos, are far too limited as interpretations of these concepts and she says this is why we find ourselves in massive, intra and inter, religious conflicts.

Over the next months as the Presbyterians of PCUSA come to grips with the logos of our current confrontations, healing hinges on exchanging our human errancies for the mythos of Christ's love.

Tuesday, September 27, 2005

To Be Considered?

As more reports are released by the Task Force (on Peace, Unity and Purity) within the Presbyterian Church USA, more resistance is generated by those adherents who would direct (they would say, retain) the denomination's tenets and polity. The terms orthodoxy, impasse and split are prevalent within Presbyterians' discussions of the denomination's current state.

In a recent committee interviewing a candidate for a church pulpit, the discussion gravitated to, "where is the denomination drifting." One person's answer was most direct - "a civil war." This observation expresses more potential than we want to accept.

The problem, however, is more complicated than we can imagine. This will not be a simple two way split with a reversion of one side to positions labeled fundamental or literal while the other side adopts positions labeled unorthodox or apostate.

Could we consider this alternative? If the Christian Church (including the Presbyterian) is to survive attrition and the current death knell conflicts, there must emerge a third sprout rooted in that universal love which finally grasps Jesus' message as beyond culture or the written; and accurately comprehends God as being beyond confinement to culture-developed or book religions.

Thursday, October 6, 2005

The Priesthood of All Believers

Over the five or so centuries of its existence as a recognizable denominational entity within Christianity, Presbyterianism has proclaimed that its individual members have a unique status within the belief system and the polity of the denomination. This is stated as - the priesthood of all believers - which declares that every Presbyterian (better - every believer) relates directly to God and to all humans with no necessity for intermediary human agents or priests.

Currently there are those Presbyterians, of the laity and of the priestly, who would deny us this universal priesthood by delimiting the terms of our relationships, to God and to one another. If, or when, one deviates from the belief patterns set by these folks their response is to label us apostate.

Let's look at it this way: If (admittedly a huge IF of course) our relationship with God and our relationships with our neighbors are rooted and growing in God's love and grace, who on Earth can better evaluate our belief systems than us? -- Why are those Presbyterian Laymen or Pastors, who would label us apostate and deny us our believer's priesthood, more orthodox than we are?

Tuesday, October 18, 2005

I Had to Lighten Up.

Last week I failed to post a blog. I apologize. I was deep into a study of the Peace, Unity, Purity Report of the 20 member Theological Task Force of the PCUSA. This week I had to come away from that study to rest my eyes and the theological tension area in my cerebral cortex.

At this point I am on the verge of drawing a conclusion. Sort of a "I think I don't know but I'm not quite sure" conclusion in keeping with the tone of the Task Force report. I'm tending to believe that 20 diverse perspectives cannot be brought to a comprehensible focus.

What if we go on a cognitive adventure and listen to some words from Mark Twain?

"We were good Presbyterian boys back there in that little Missouri town, and we all knew as strict Calvinists that if a boy committed a sin it meant the extermination of the whole countryside, cattle and all. It is in my later years that I have concluded that John Calvin may have gotten some things right but he missed the boat on the two most important aspects of life. I've found the Deity to be much kinder than Calvin allowed and I find the human to be more worthy than Calvin could bring himself to permit."

Would it be heresy to substitute the phrase "Book of Order" for the word "Calvin" in the previous quote?"

Do you suppose that we Presbyterians take ourselves too seriously? Could we substitute "getting to be religious" for the phrase "getting to be seventy" in the following Twain quote?

"Well, when you get to be seventy. . . when you get to that advanced age, you are supposed to sit up there on that seven-terraced summit and tell the rest of the world how you got up there. They all do it, you know, all these garrulous old people. They explain the process and dwell on the particulars with senile rapture. I think I achieved my seventy years in the usual way; by sticking strictly to a scheme of life that would kill anyone else. The point I want to make is that you can't reach old age by another person's road. My habits protect my life but they'd probably assassinate you. You have to make up your own rules and then stick to them. That's not as easy as it sounds, either, because there's bound to be somebody trying to reform you, trying to take all the pleasure right out of your life and replace it with dreariness. But don't let them ! If you can't make seventy by a comfortable road, don't go!"

15

Saturday, November 19, 2005

Innocent Errancies

The Presbyterian Church in the United States of America, PCUSA, is preparing for internal confrontations over accepting, or not accepting, the report from its Theology Task Force, TTF.

This task force made up of 20 diverse members of the church was selected in 2001 to study the Peace, Unity and Purity, PUP, of the Church and render a report to its General Assembly on what the task force discerned to be a solution to the conflicts within the church with reference to the ordination of persons of homosexual orientation.

It is my discernment that the report, a conscientious product of twenty persons who grew into the loving acceptance of each other as diverse individuals, will not be acceptable within the Right/Wrong current climate of the PCUSA.

This climate exists because the Church is stunted by innocent errancies. In my recent book, A Belief System from the General Store, I list innocent errancy in the glossary as: "a coined term to express the state of believing errant information innocently because it is the best information currently available. e.g. The world is flat (1491), the Biblical creation stories, the early concept that the sun rotates around the earth."

As we come to realize how our innocent errancies stultify our belief systems, our expanding concepts of God will lead us beyond seeing others as right or wrong to reasoning with others as we seek the truth, not my truth or your truth -- God's truth.

Wednesday, January 11, 2006

Catechism

Early in the eighth decade of my life, when I finally acknowledged that every person's belief system should be self scrutinized, I wrote a little book.*

As a part of this book I reworked the Shorter Catechism to align its content with the culture of the 21st Century rather than that of the 17th Century, in which the Catechism originated.

In a discussion group comprised of Traditionalists and (Neo?) Traditionalists, delving into this 21st Century Catechism, we explored the generic nature of catechisms and then zeroed in on the first one as a specific comparative exercise.

Exhibit A. 17th Century Shorter Catechism, Question #1:
Q. 1. What is the chief end of man?
A. 1. Man's chief end is to glorify God, and enjoy him forever.

Exhibit B. 21st Century Shorter Catechism, Question #1:
Q. 1. What is the primary purpose of the human?
A. 1. The primary purpose of the human is to be response-able to God's Being in order to fulfill that human's being and to help others fulfill theirs.

(Note. If I were composing a modification of this catechism today I would forego the concept of God having "being." God having being is an anthropomorphic error.)

One discussant was not sure if the term response-able placed intended demands on the human, beyond the word responsible.

A summary of our conclusions determined that all animals fill responsible niches in the Earth's nature but that only the human animal is response-able to the God of the Universe, the Ground of All Being.

A second member of the group posed this astute question:

"Are there gradations of fulfilling one's being? If so how, or does, God evaluate from failure through ordinary to excellence? What is wrong with ordinary?"

Seems to me this query approaches the ultimate catechism which consists of two questions:

Q. 1. Do religions exist because the human searches for guides to achieving at least an ordinary quality of life?
A. 1. Yes.

Q. 2. Do religions exist because the human searches for a means of achieving some everlasting spiritual state?
A. 2. Yes.

Where, then, do religions really come from?

If God is Love. If God is Grace.
If Love is real. If Grace is true.
Who will deny salvation to the many,
And proclaim it for the few?*

*"A Belief System from the General Store"

Thursday, January 26, 2006

Belief Systems and Baling Wire

I grew up on a farm behind a general store next to a country church - a long time ago. I rate these three locales among the best learning environments on this earth:

The farm for learning basic survival.
The store for learning how society functions.
The church for learning spiritual relationships.

Murphy's Law: If anything can go wrong, it will.
The Farmer's Corollary: For this God gave us baling wire.
The Storekeeper's Adage: Honesty is the best policy.
The Church's Creed: Christ's Sermon on the Mount.*

During my early, formative years my belief system was shaped and molded by the cultures of the three environments listed above. My subsequent environments changed more rapidly than my belief system. I still believe that God provides baling wire for when things go wrong, that honesty is always best in the long run, that the Sermon on the Mount is a one-size-fits-all message.

I learned on the farm that experience is recognizing a mistake the second time you make it. I heeded the admonitions of the loafers at the store, "We have to profit from the mistakes of others - we're not going to live long enough to make all of them ourselves."

But now I find that the Christian Church is not keeping pace with the changing world. Knowledge has taken us beyond many previous suppositions: the earth is not flat; the sun does not revolve around the earth; the two Biblical myths of creation cannot be taken literally.

I am not alone. More and more ordinary believers, like me, find themselves struggling with the beliefs of the present Christian Church. More and more the Church clings dogmatically to beliefs that developed in a world far different from the one in which we now live.

Certain mysteries and Biblical revelations are so counterintuitive that they make belief difficult. I shall name but one. God came into a specific culture of humans as a divine human manifestation who had to die to save all human cultures of all time from intrinsic behaviors, termed sin, of which they were/are preeminently capable. This portion of the Christian Belief System is difficult for many to comprehend. When we are asked to arrive at this belief sequence via a concept known as the Fall - many find it to be impossible.

Although I can speak only to my struggles, I suspect there are others who share the same or similar struggles, hence I shall be bold to use the personal pronoun, we, rather than I.

We bear witness to those comprehensions of God that we believe to be consistent with the natural and spiritual possibilities of existence. We honor all mysteries, so long as they acknowledge God as the ground of all being and all humans as response able to God. We honor all humans as fellow humans, though many claim differing, or no, comprehensions of God.

We believe that our comprehensions can derive from Jesus of Nazareth without endorsing as inerrant all statements of the Bible and by the Past and Present Christian Church.

We believe that the Christian Church must change.

We hear it being said, "The Christian Church must change or it will die."

We concur with that extenuation, and yet. . . could the following express more accurately what we hope for?

"The Christian Church must change so that it can live more fully through the lives of more and more persons."

Bishop John Shelby Spong states: "the Sermon on the Mount is a beautifully crafted piece of work based on Psalm 119, a hymn to the beauty and wonder of the Torah, which was used by the Jews as part of a 24 hour vigil called Shavuot."

Sunday, March 19, 2006

Beyond Baling Wire

The Denominational Church in which my belief system is on deposit is the Presbyterian Church USA. The PCUSA is currently in the throes of change. Segments within the denomination are in adversarial struggles over their basics of belief which they term: core beliefs, tenets, doctrines, etc. to which they have applied the short hand term - The Peace, Unity and Purity of the Church.

The 213th General Assembly (2001) of the PCUSA established a Theological Task Force to study the Peace, Unity and Purity of the Church. That Task Force has completed its Final Report and will present its recommendations to the 217th General assembly (2006).

This Task Force exercise is an honest attempt to solve a serious problem - with baling wire. The report consumes a 50-page booklet. The recommendations, associated rationales and final words subsume 13 of those pages. In addition to this material a later press .release from PCUSA News containing 21 printout pages of e-mail gives the reader the unabridged, unedited, personal observations and conclusions of the 20 members of the Task Force. The booklet is a copious accumulation of pedantic, baling wire material. The e-mail pages contain sprinkles of compassion and genius from beyond baling wire.

If General Assembly can somehow transfer that material found beyond the baling wire to the hearts and minds of the PCUSA membership -- it may save the church from schism.

Thursday, April 27, 2006

Why Do Good People Do Inappropriate Things?

Inappropriate behavior is refusing to learn from the effects of inappropriate behavior.

Tuesday, June 6, 2006

We Have Moved.

Elinor and I Have Moved.
This seems a strange heading for a blog.

The deeper we get into the process, the more it seems a strange thing to do.

A while ago we started thinking toward moving into a retirement community. Thinking turned to planning, and planning turned to doing. In Spring, 2006 we changed our Salem address of some 54 years to Meadowood Retirement Community, 2455 Tamarack Trail, Apt. 113, Bloomington, IN 47408. Changing an address is one thing. Changing our physical location is quite another.

It was fairly easy to have two husky young men from - A Better Way, Moving and Storage - load some furniture and furnishings into a moving van and wave them off to Bloomington. It was even easier to wave them on their way with what proved to be an excess of worldly goods.

Now comes the difficult (actually the impossible): sort through 54 years of stuff from the house we built in 1952, end up compressed with some of it in an apartment and be freed from the rest.

Our six children came to the homestead (from all over the U.S. plus Australia) for a week in May, 2006, dug out all the artifacts, sorted them, chose far too few as their inheritances, and prepared the remainder for an Auction - July 1. I retract the previous statement about "actually the impossible" - they removed im from impossible. They proved that with God, plus the right six children, "all things are possible."

Over the years I have not been too worried about the Tenth Commandment, "Thou shalt not covet." Especially since it extended the definition of covet to include such farfetched things as: "your neighbor's house, his wife, his manservant, or his maid servant, his ox, or his ass, or anything else that is your neighbor's." It is only now that I realize how desperately serious the commandment would be if it had stated, "Thou shalt not covet, period."

I'm not sure what the difference is between collecting and coveting. I sure do hope that in the Big Book of Deeds, God's Secretary lists Elinor and me as collectors.

Wednesday June 21, 2006

Can One Be Religious Without Being Tiring?

This might be the most difficult question within the realm of religion.

But please do not answer it yet. Struggle with it after you have pondered these two preliminary questions.

    1. What must one do to be human?

    2. What must one believe to be religious?

How do you define being human? being religious? Where do you stand in the debate on faith and works?

Let's not bring sources into the study yet. Could you be religious without telling other humans about it - even to the point of tiring them?

I'm going to think about these questions for a few days and then start putting my thoughts into blogs. Why don't you share in this process?

Saturday, June 24, 2006

Is Religion Instinctual Action or Intellectual Decision?

I've pondered the two questions given in the June 21, 2006 blog. I have even modified question number 1.

    1. What must one be/do to be human? (Note how I have broadened the question).

    2. What must one believe to be religious?

The answer to the first question is an admission.
The answer to the second is a commission.

The admission is that we are animals. There is irrefutable anatomical evidence that homo sapiens bears visible structural relationships to the other animals. DNA studies confirm irrefutable, invisible evidence that homo sapiens is more closely related to some animals than to others.

Here we are. How we came to be is not yet a part of the question.

How do we differ from the other animals? We at least differ from even the higher orders of animals in balance - the balance between instinctual actions and intellectual decisions.

Other animal species possess varying degrees of instinctual capabilities and minimal intellectual abilities. The human possesses amazing intellect but very rudimentary instinctual capabilities.

To be human the individual must utilize his/her intellect. Because intellect is a universal human trait the first utilization of intellect is to respect all others who possess it.

Thus we arrive at commission. If we are to respect our humanity we must commit to respecting the humanity of our fellow humans, and the entirety of the nature that accepts and sustains us. Could this be rudimentary religion? If so, is religion instinctual or intellectual?

To be continued.

Tuesday, July 04, 2006

What is The Basis?

In my current series of blogs I am creeping up (slowly) on two questions -
    1. What must one be/do to be human?
    2. What must one believe/do to be religious?

This morning in the shower (thinking, singing, whistling are all good ways to transform a chore such as a shower into an experience) the thought came to me that there are two prior questions to the two listed above.

01. What authenticates one to answer these questions?
02. Why should those answers deserve credence?

I believe that I have given sufficient answer to question 02. in the June 24, 2006 blog via the following statement:

"To be human the individual must utilize his/her intellect. Because intellect is a universal human trait the first utilization of intellect is to respect all others who possess it."

Today is Independence Day. What an appropriate day to consider question 01.

Since the traits of humanness and religiousness cannot be measured by any scientific means and since they have evolved and are evolving over such immense periods of time, how do we evaluate specific humans who give answers, and the answers they give?

We can evaluate their person hood by their fulfillment of that respect for their humankind that is the basis of their being human.

We can evaluate their answers by what positive or negative effects those answers have as a basis for communal respect.

And here we arrive at religion. If it is instinctual there must be a basis for that instinct. If it is intellectual there must be a basis for that intellect. Whatever form that basis takes it must come from outside the human even though it somehow exists within the human. Ancients named this basis God. Might we be more direct and just capitalize the b in Basis. Tillich said God is the ground of all being. Why can't we say Basis is the ground of all being.

Why would some ancients' answers be more valid than those of extant humans?

If The Basis is Grace, if Grace is fair, would The Basis choose some humans as more authentic than others?

I'll give you a week and a few showers to work on that.

25

Monday, July 17, 2006

They Aren't

July 17 has rolled around much quicker than I anticipated. Last blog I left us hanging with this question:

If The Basis is Grace, if Grace is fair, would The Basis choose some humans as more authentic than others?

As better stated it is this:

"Why would some ancients' answers be more valid than those of extant humans?"

In the intervening time I read the following in an article defending the doctrine of the Trinity and its paternalistic nature:

"God has named himself and likes his name."

Thus far I have avoided quoting proof texts. but at this point an irresistible quote comes to mind. Mark Twain said: "Man is the noblest work of God. Now I wonder who found that out."

Now how did the Trinity defender find out that God has named himself and is pleased with his name?

The age-old explanation that it is through divine revelation sure does put the concept that God is Grace in a tight corner, doesn't it? The theological way out of the corner is to make another anthropomorphic observation; God chooses to reveal God's Grace as God chooses. Does that mean that God is sometimes Grace and sometimes not Grace?

Seems to me that The Basis of all being is not so finite as to be defined by individuals (after all "define" is what divine revelation does) in specific blips of time. The Basis of all being is so infinite and indefinable that the human should be content with the knowledge that there is A Basis for the primary human utilization of intellect which is to respect all others who possess it.

Is "to define the divine" an oxymoron?

How can humans relate to their unseen Basis if they do not utilize their intellects to relate to the seen fellow human?

So what is my answer to the question, "Why would some ancients' answers be more valid than those of extant humans?"

Seems to me the only logical answer is - They aren't.

Monday, July 24, 2006

Did GOD name HIMself?

I just can't get over someone making the presumptive statement: "The Triune God has named himself, and he likes his name." Eventually I'll wear out on it and get over it.

So what does the Triune God "think" of the names Yahweh and Allah? Put another way, what do Yahweh and Allah "think" of the name Triune God?

Do the anthropomorphic words, likes and think, as used above, render human writings questionable?

Seems to me that countless adherents of all faiths have so taken the Lord's name in vain that the Almighty might welcome a new name.

Would some other human then say? "God has renamed himself and likes his new name."

Sunday, August 13, 2006

Instinctual and Maturing Religion

Today in the shower two thoughts came into my mind at the same time. This is cause for panic because my mind is structured for only one thought at a time.

Thought 1. There is a Basis (God) for all Being.

Thought 2. When intellect came into being how did/does intellect recognize God?

In an earlier blog I casually spelled out, with no claim of divine revelation, this premise:

"God is so infinite and indefinable that the human should be content with the knowledge that there is A Basis for the primary human utilization of intellect which is to respect all others who possess it."

I do believe that there is a pinch of response-able Spirit in every human. Physical form is only part of being human. The Pinch is what defines humanity. It is as we utilize this pinch (not as the pinch directs us - many readers will differ) that we utilize the intellect that produces our respect for the intellects of others.

Right here I acknowledge that free will is more comprehensible to me than foreordination. I can't speak for God but for me there seems more practicality in self-winding watches than in those that must be wound by a Divine Winder.

When each human of every generation was/is born the Pinch first comes into play as assisting that human's intellect to relate to and respect other humans' intellects. Perhaps this could be termed Instinctual Religion? (Relating to God and Nature come to the individual later. Perhaps this could be termed Maturing Religion?)

Later as the Pinch foreordains the individual to utilize his/her free will by being response-able to God, maturing religion leads the individual to not only relate to but to be responsible to/for fellow humans and the rest of nature.

I cannot explain the intricate workings of foreordination and free will, nor the workings of Instinctual Religion and Maturing Religion. My hope is that we can bring our intellectual powers to bear on them in ways other than via the anthropomorphic terms that we are so prone to use.

Tuesday, August 29, 2006

Anthropomorphic or Cosmic

See the August 13 blog. What do we mean by anthropomorphic terms?

Anthropomorphism is the noun that gives human form and/or behavior to bears or monkeys or God. The adjective anthropomorphic thus describes whatever we apply an anthropomorphism to. Does God think? Think is an anthropomorphic term when applied to God. We can not know whether God thinks or not. The cosmos is evidence that there has been/is function. That function is so complex that "think" is an absolutely inadequate term to describe this cosmic function. Whether this function is God or The Cosmic Functionary, the name is not the issue of this moment.

The human needs to use its intellect to be human rather than to obsess on how the intellect came to be. Sort of like the fellow who had this epithet carved on his tombstone: "Thank God I could be an atheist."

Assigning intelligence to the Cosmic Functionary is anthropomorphic. The same goes for the terms design or designer. I am all for finding out that man can be noble - not necessarily that man is the noblest work of God. I am all for finding out what embryonic stem cells that are going to be destroyed can contribute to preventing or curing human catastrophes. I am all for thanking whatever force and whatever means brought the presence of human intellect. I am all for thanking our remote ancestors for being curious about their beginnings.

Their mythical assumptions relative to the creation of the all in all of life visible to them were remarkable though maximally anthropomorphic and minimally cosmic. Therefore, I resist becoming stuck in their clay and spittle creation of the human and their six day, Biblical, anthropomorphic explanation of the all of creation.

Logical science is basic to the cosmos. Mythical assumptions are human additions. The dilemma throughout the existence of human intellect is that the human is capable of extrapolating both – logical science and mythical assumptions.

Tuesday, January 23, 2007

God Is The Atmosphere Of Possibilities

Just as my current series of blogs was straining toward confronting the jargon-like term "Intelligent Design," Serendipity tapped me on the shoulder and held out a bright yellow book titled "Genes, Genesis and God, Their Origins in Natural and Human History" by Holmes Rolston, III.

First I must express my thanks to my friend Rudy Rudolph who loaned the book and flattered me by assuming that I could understand the author's thesis. Next I must thank the author for utilizing enough elementary terms within his much more complicated thesis to permit me onto his cognitive wavelength.

I quote Rolston (p.367):

"The divine spirit is the giver of life, pervasively present over the millennia. God is the atmosphere of possibilities, the metaphysical environment, in, with, and under first the natural and later also the cultural environment, luring the Earthen histories upslope."

"God is the atmosphere of possibilities, the metaphysical environment . . . "

God is the Cosmic Functionary, that life giving atmosphere of possibilities, which includes as one of its many processes that through which the human animal with its unique cosmic pinch develops physically, intellectually and metaphysically with and within cosmic reality and metaphysical suprareality.

When we think cosmically of God as the Infinite Provider of ALL processes, ALL THAT IS, as opposed to anthropomorphically as the finite creator of the limited process of evolving the human, we will realize how micro the word evolution is, and how inappropriate the anthropomorphic term Intelligent Design is, within the Macro Cosmos.

I personally have extreme difficulty thinking beyond my humanity. For example: whatever the size the glob of light matter and dark matter was that is now ever expanding after the big bang, I lose all sense of explanation if the word Creator is inserted followed by a question mark. I am much more comfortable with the word Provider (as of process) and then a question mark. Perhaps if we use the objective term, evolutionary process, in our studies rather than the possessive term, Darwin's Theory, we could have more constructive dialogue.

To utilize Dr. Rolston's previously stated metaphor:

"God is the atmosphere of possibilities, the metaphysical environment . . ."

In that light could we state that:

The Cosmic Functionary is atmospheric (all life giving) not anthropomorphic (human imitating).

Within the current dilemma, could it be that the term Intelligent Design is an anthropomorphic diversion creating a debilitating waste of human energy within the atmospheric reality and metaphysical suprareality?

Monday, February 05, 2007

Tenets

My current beliefs differ from those prescribed within the traditional path that brought me to them. Does this mean that I am ineligible for a leap of faith? Soren Kierkegarrd concluded that though we follow a path to reach it, our ultimate belief system requires a leap of faith.

C.S. Lewis argues against the leap and states that a belief in the Supernatural, the basic tenet essential to Christianity, can be inferred from teleological sources of human reason. Whether faith comes through a leap or through a teleological inference, the church, in fact all of religion, asserts that the acceptance of certain tenets (doctrines) is essential to the authentication of that faith. Though humans are in the cosmos they desire to connect to something supernatural to all that is cosmic (a force differing from the laws of nature). The primal question of all religion: What essential tenet(s) must its adherents follow so that the human spirit (a pinch of the supernatural) shall be retained within (saved by) this Cosmic Force?

Interestingly, the current issue of The Presbyterian Outlook, January 29, 2007, has a commentary on page 12 left, "What Ails the Church?" while the facing page 13 right carries an article titled, "Essential Tenets?" Many suspect that what ails the church is too many controversial, essential tenets - tenets that are either too ambiguous or too rigid when relating the natural to differing concepts of the supernatural.

The church (e.g. a denomination) seeks to fulfill the basic tenet, how it delineates and relates to its concept of the Supernatural Cosmic Force (e.g. God), by developing innumerable essential tenets through which its members shall connect to God.

All of these tenets were/are developed by humans and presented in human language. Some tenets go back 4,000 years and are recorded in the Bible. These are deemed inspired and authentic because it is claimed by subsequent humans that God had a special, inspirational relationship with those earlier humans.

To continue this premise of inspiration, tenets developed since the Biblical Canon was closed are deemed authentic if somehow they can justify, or be justified by, this established Scripture.

In his book "Genes, Genesis and God, Their Origins in Natural and Human History," Dr. Holmes Rolston, III states succinctly where the leap of faith will take us, and where it has taken human cultures. I quote Dr. Rolston (p.367):

"The divine spirit is the giver of life, pervasively present over the millennia. God is the atmosphere of possibilities, the metaphysical environment, in, with, and under first the natural and later also the cultural environment, luring the Earthen histories upslope."

My path toward a belief system, my leap of faith into the atmosphere of possibilities, the metaphysical environment, is a bruising exercise because I impact against so many barricades with the words "Essential Tenet" emblazoned upon them.

Addendum:

Here I present two lists of suggested essential tenets from the article noted above ("Essential Tenets?" Presbyterian Outlook, January 29, 2007) by Joseph D. Small, Director of the office of Theology, Worship and Education, Presbyterian Church (USA) and a core member of Re-Forming Ministry.)

List A.

Joseph D. Small states - "Some Presbyterians suggest that essential tenets can be inferred from the ordination vows themselves. The list of necessary doctrines would then include: (1) the Trinity (2) several Christological affirmations (3) the authority of Scriptures (4) the reliability of the church's confessions as guides to belief and action (5) adherence to the church's polity and discipline (6) obedient discipleship (7) an ecumenically principled ecclesiology and (8) a particular understanding of ministry."

List B.

Rev. Small states further that others may propose that Chapter II of the Book of Order, Presbyterian Church (USA), yields a constitutionally credible list of essential tenets: "(1) the Trinity (2) the incarnation (3) grace alone, faith alone (4) the sovereignty of God (5) election (6) covenantal ecclesiology (7) stewardship and (8) the necessity to transform societies."

As we take the leap of faith are we supported by or are we confused by the plethora of tenets and the super plethora of tenet interpretations - from the past and from the present?

This confuses me. Might it ail the church?

Thursday, March 15, 2007

Amazing

An amazing thing happened to the last blog, titled "Tenets," that I posted on February 5, 2007. It seemed to fit the mold of a Letter to the Editor. In a moment of hope I postal mailed it to The Presbyterian Outlook, the magazine that contained the articles it quoted.

An e-mail from the Editor came back immediately, "Could I send it to them as an electronic message so that it would save them retyping it?" Of course I could. I did.

First they posted it on their web site and later, as a Letter to the Editor, in the hard copy volume of The Presbyterian Outlook published March 5, 2007.

Not from the ego of having it published, but from the humble thanks for having it shared, I am encouraged to hope that others see merit in expanding on the thoughts that it may contribute toward a solution to "What Ails the Church?"

What ails religion? the Church? the PCUSA?
Who defines the ailment?
Can essential tenets solve human differences and dilemmas?
Have they ever?
What prescription might cure this ailment?
Who can compound such a prescription?

Presbyterians can define, compound, cure, and, yes, heal if they will go up to the mountain and, like Martin Luther King, Jr., look over and see the promised land.

But the trail up the mountain is humbling. We must forego ego. We must empty ourselves of centuries of pride and prejudice. We must unlearn traditions. We must question essential tenets.

Not only is the trail up the mountain humbling but man has attained the capability of destroying all trails, even all life on the Earth. In the words of Einstein:

"The unleashed power of the atom has changed everything except our thinking. Thus we are drifting toward a change beyond conception. We shall require a substantially different way of thinking if mankind is to survive."

Not only the unleashed misuse of the atom but the uncontrolled abuse of religion can bring changes beyond conception. We must totally change our way of thinking:

- about the Cosmos,
- about the nature of life within the Cosmos,
- about The Supernatural Force within/without the Cosmos.

Wednesday, March 21, 2007

The To-Be-Known Land

Probably none of us will equal the efforts of Martin Luther King, Jr. but each of us is obliged to go up the mountain - if the ailing church is to recover. The difficulty is that we cannot go up the mountain unless we leave behind the cumbersome traditions and securities of the ailing church as we climb to the crest to look over and behold the promised land, the to-be-known land.

Much within the real and natural is truly known. Much is still conjecture. Much within the spiritual and metaphysical is stated to be known by many temporal human minds, although dimly. When minds become eternal (as fulfilled human pinches of Cosmic Spirit) they will know, and then more clearly. This is not original. It is Paul.

If my trail of faith has brought me to a leap into "the atmosphere of possibilities, the metaphysical environment," (Ralston, Genes, Genesis and God) which "lures humans, cultures and the Earthen histories upslope," how do I determine if that into which I leap is authentic?

1. Is it authentic because specific other humans (through tradition, books, councils, institutions, canons, tenets, etc.) have declared it to be? Have some humans received special insights (revelations) from that which they conceive to be the Spiritual Force within/without the Cosmos?

2. Is it authentic because I assume, believe, or "know" it to be?

If we make either of these claims, what then are our concepts of Grace? Might we be unduly self centered? Might our claims render our God too small?

As I climb the mountain hoping for a view of the promised land, I find that many traditions have become barricades and previous security blankets are now straight jackets. What do I retain and what do I discard? Will my fellows reject me as I cast aside old, restrictive tenets and absorb new, diverse perspectives. My changes will be authentic and accepted only if they respect all others I meet, within the humbleness of love. Religions are conceived by humans searching for a relation with the Cosmic Spiritual Force plus meaning for their lives. Religions fail when they would force their beliefs on others. Religions succeed when they demonstrate the true force, that being love - love so easy to proclaim, so difficult to produce.

Mark Twain warns about humans devoid of love:

"Such can be the human race. Often it does seem a pity that Noah and his party did not miss the boat."

Thursday, March 29, 2007

Preparing for the Climb

Come, let us reason together. What will be needed to climb the mountain?

It seems to me that climbing the mountain is a metaphor for constructing a belief system that serves as a platform for Kierkegarrd's leap of faith or for finding C.S. Lewis' Cosmic Source of teleological reasoning. Whichever suits the searcher best, it will take strength to achieve it.

Does the church provide those strengths? YES and NO. In spite of centuries of exhausting, conscientious effort the answer can only be - yes and no. Why this schismatic answer?

The church has struggled through its centuries to provide truth to its adherents.

    A. Predominantly the church has followed the subjective model. Once some myth or doctrine or tenet has been ruled true through the claim of revelation, tradition, or practice the institutional church presses it upon its members as subjective truth. Could this result in pseudo strength?

    B. Occasionally some church bodies have followed the objective model. The members are given the opportunity to develop belief systems which derive from perceiving what gives the most meaning to their lives and the greatest common good to all their relationships. Could this lead to inherent strength?

On my climb* it will be necessary for me to have criteria by which I can select the tools and trails which fulfill my climb. My criteria for these selections shall be twofold:

1. Stewardship. I shall be response-able to that Cosmic Force which shares with me a pinch of this Force and gives me the intellect to comprehend the meaning of life.

2. Fellowship. I shall show responsibility for my pinch and my intellect by respecting other climbers, all of whom have the pinch and intellect, as we make the common good our primary purpose of life.

Where will I find catalogs of the climbing tools and maps for the trails?

I'll start that search next week.

my climb. I shall use the first person pronoun or the neutral (hope-fully objective) third person. The reader is under no pressure to concur with the material expressed.

Thursday, April 05, 2007

My Climb

I believe there is a Cosmic Force "luring the Earthen histories upslope" (Rolston).

I believe this is the Cosmic God luring me up the mountain.

My plan is to select a tiny sliver from the religions' pie chart, the Presbyterian Church in the United States of America (PCUSA), seek to discover its tenets, determine if these tenets qualify as Tenets for Cosmic Stewardship and Common Good Fellowship, then discern their effectiveness as instructions (tools) for the average Presbyterian climber.

Chapter II of the Book of Government within the Constitution of the PCUSA contains a facile listing of items which individually fit the definition of tenets and collectively present a definitive Faith Statement. (1) the Trinity (2) the Incarnation (3) Grace alone, Faith alone, Scriptures alone (4) the Sovereignty of God (5) Election (6) the Covenantal life (7) Stewardship (8) the Transformation of societies.

This list is not exhaustive, of course, nor could it possibly meet the thinking of all Presbyterians. Its major strength is the fact that it has maintained a position of Constitutionality over the centuries of the Presbyterian Church as a studying and testing institution. Therefore it seems to be a plausible, fair, broad based list to study in establishing the tools and trails for an average Presbyterian climber.

In my last week's blog I named two criteria which I believe qualify a tenet to be essential or vital to all of life including the climb.

1. Stewardship. Will the tenet help me be a response-able steward to that Cosmic Force which shares with me a pinch of this Force and gives me the intellect to comprehend the meaning of life as my primary purpose?
2. Fellowship. Will the tenet help me show responsibility for my pinch and my intellect by respecting other climbers, all of whom have the pinch and intellect, as we make the common good our secondary purpose of life?

Next week we will go through the list of eight tenets one by one for answers.

Thursday, April 12, 2007

Sequencing My Tenet

My climb is not a solo effort. We all need help from personal others. We need help from corporate others. We need that support which comes through the auspices of communal groups. My group is the Presbyterian Church. It is with humble temerity (a contradiction of terms) that I would suggest, as an average church member in the 21st Century, some tenet reforms wherein my church could strengthen my climb and smooth my trails up the mountain.

As noted in the April 5, 2007 blog, a review of the eight tenets listed there will not be sufficient for some readers, but I hope that my comfort with this list does not deprive me of my status of average.

I am sure that there was no attempt to attain order (of rank or chronology) as the eight were incorporated into the Presbyterian Constitution. However, I find the order of listing awkward as I attempt to discern how each tenet will function as an assist or as a deterrent to my climb.

Therefore I shall discuss them in the following order: (1) the Sovereignty of God (2) Election (3) Stewardship (4) the Covenantal life (5) the Transformation of Societies (6) Scriptures alone, Grace alone, Faith alone (7) the Incarnation (8) the Trinity.

1. The Sovereignty of God.

I find difficulty with this term on two counts - first what it says - and second what it does not say.

What it says: It immediately limits God by imposing the human term sovereign - ruler, monarch, head of state . . . . and thus reduces God anthropomorphically. In the times when this term was coined it connoted much more ultimacy than it does in the 21st Century. We now have an entirely different concept of ultimacy as we explore the vastness of the cosmos.

What it does not say: It does not say that God is undefinable and incomprehensible. It does not say that we humans must think in expansive, beyond human, terms of God as the Force within/without the entirety of the cosmos.

It does not say that God is so incomprehensible that applying human traits to God: male, female, patriarchal, matriarchal, sovereign, thinks, acts, speaks, promises . . . diminishes God.

Yes, this tenet is essential to my climb. However, I'll change it from God is Sovereign to God is Cosmic. No, better still, I'll just say -- God Is.

Tuesday, April 17, 2007

Tenet 2. Election

Tenet 1. God Is.
Tenet 2. Election.

In the Book of Order the statement -
"The election of the people of God for service as well as for salvation;" is listed as one of the great themes of the reformed tradition. I concur that this is indeed a theme that could transpose into an essential tenet for my climb.

However, within this transposition, a question comes to mind. Would this statement have been a more effective reforming theme if framed in these words? "The election of all humans for service as well as for salvation."

Does speaking of "the people of God" infer that there are those people who are not "of God?" For a brief period I tried participating in friendly (a misnomer) chat rooms conducted on the internet for pastors and lay people by various groups within our denomination. I quickly became disillusioned and withdrew because of the bitter exchanges relative to - "who are, and who are not, children of God, people of God?"

Within the undefinable Image of God as the Within/Without Cosmic Force, the human being has evolved to the possessing of intellect. The basic sign of intellect is the human ability to recognize that fellow humans have intellect.

Within the incomprehensible Spirit of God as the Within/Without Cosmic Force, a pinch of that spirit devolves to every human being. This pinch renders every human response-able to God and responsible to every other human.

If we humans cannot define or comprehend God why do we think that we can restrict (diminish) God when we determine those whom God elects "for service as well as salvation?"

The communal (common good) history of humankind, from its evolution to intellect to the devolution of the pinch, from its Judeo roots to its Christian branches, and in all its religions and societies, has been compromised by the misuse of the words - election and chosen.

As we climb we do not want to berate others by claiming that we alone are God's elect, nor do we want to be berated by those who claim to be God's sole elect.

Tenet 2. Election - can be essential and can make my climb smoother if I recognize that being human and being elect are synonymous.

Friday, April 20, 2007

Tenet 3. Stewardship

Tenet 1. God is.
Tenet 2. God elects every human.
Tenet 3. Every human is response-able (a steward) to God.

The human can say, "I do not believe God is."
The human can say, "I do not believe God elects every human."
These doubting statements do not render the first two tenets false any more than affirming statements can make them true. These two are truly Leap of Faith or Teleological Belief tenets. Humans may generate (or contaminate) the religion zones in their brains by discussing (or arguing) these two matters, but at the end of the day the human simply cannot claim ownership or definability of these two basic tenets.

Tenet 3. is different.

In the Book of Order; great themes of the Reformed tradition include:

"A faithful stewardship that shuns ostentation and seeks proper use of the gifts of God's creation." Please remember the word ostentation. It will appear later.

The human does hold ownership of this third tenet. Here we shift from believing the climb has purpose to actually climbing. Here the human becomes response-able to use the first two tenets listed above as a backpack for multiple stewardship tools.

Just as the word election has suffered misuse the word stewardship has suffered insufficient use. It does have one shortcoming. As the term sovereign God implies a human status to God so steward indicates a subservient relationship to the human. But, while the term sovereign diminishes God, the term steward enhances the human.

In that light stewardship to God is the ultimate role for humans as they seek meaning for life. What about worship? How better to worship God than to protect God's Earth and Cosmos?

What about fellowship? How better to commune with God than to commune with our fellow stewards? Stewardship within our climb is more about loving than about giving or receiving.

Stewardship is an essential tenet and the flagship tenet of being response-able humans.

Thursday, April 26, 2007

Tenet 4. Covenant Life

1. God is.
2. Election is God's.
3. Stewardship is every human's.

4. Covenantal Life and the Common Good.

In the Book of Order; great themes of the Reformed tradition include:

"Covenant life marked by a disciplined concern for order in the church according to the word of God."

This is a specific denomination making a statement in its Constitution. However I find it restrictive as I climb the mountain alongside fellow humans of many beliefs. I recognize that I climb under the auspices and concerned order of the Presbyterian Church but I hope to covenant with all my fellow climbers in a common good relationship. A relationship wherein God is not bound or restricted by a specific book defined as THE Word of God.

I always find the term, the Scripture, the word of God, intriguing yet discouraging. When I went to Wickipedia to research the term the following chapter appeared:

"The General Assembly of the Northern Presbyterian Church in 1910 affirmed five essential doctrines regarded as under attack in the church: the inerrancy of Scripture, the Virgin Birth, the Substitutionary Atonement of Christ, Christ's bodily resurrection, and the historicity of the miracles. These were reaffirmed in 1916 and 1923. Another version put the Deity of Christ in place of the Virgin Birth."

"The inerrancy of Scripture," was the very first essential doctrine listed in 1910 as being under "attack." I do not think attack is the correct word. This infers that questioning a human concept is an attack on God. I do not suggest a confrontation over terms or a contest of beliefs. I suggest serious, prayerful study across the breadth of the church of what we are saying when we proclaim that: "we have the Word of God and it is Inerrant."

I find climbing the mountain difficult. I find establishing a covenant for the common good with my fellow climbers difficult. I find that some of the stated beliefs of my church, originally intended to support the Kingdom of God, now serve as distractions to the Kindom of God.

On the mountain I shall hope to share those Scriptures that enhance a covenant life for the common good within God's Kindom.

Monday, April 30, 2007

Tenet 5. Transformation

Tenet 1. God is.
Tenet 2. God elects every human.
Tenet 3. Every human is response-able (a steward) to God.
Tenet 4. Covenantal Life and the Common Good.
Tenet 5. The Ongoing Transformation of all Societies.

The God that is elects all of us to find meaning for our lives, to be response-able stewards, to covenant with others for the common good and to seek the transformation of societies.

The Book of Order statement G-2.500a(4) on transforming society is long and of tedious grammatical construction:

> *"(4) the recognition of the human tendency to idolatry and tyranny, which calls the people of God to work for the transformation of society by seeking justice and living in obedience to the word of God."*

In spite of claiming just previously,

G-2.500a(3), the stewardship that "shuns ostentation" the Book of Order themes of reform fall prey in this statement (4) to the ostentatious terms "the people of God" and "the word of God."

Transforming society is especially difficult when we fail to recognize that society is generally a plural noun. Apparently God does not elect all humans to be in a single society. God obviously accepts humans in societies. This is an especially difficult arrangement for: Buddhists, Christians, Hindus, Jews, Muslims, etc. as well as North Americans, South Americans, Asians, Africans, Australians,

Europeans, plus Black, Brown and White peoples, and, of all things, conservatives or liberals ... to comprehend.

Born and raised with literal suspenders and a bible belt it has come as quite a surprise to me that Cosmic God permits me to modify, even reject, some of the tenets that certain Christian Societies insist are essential to keeping me clothed in God's acceptance.

Just as the reformers could reject ostentation in one tenet and be ostentatious in the next, tenets are made by humans and may contain contradictions.

I am uncomfortable with the reform term "transformation of society," which seems to me to infer "the church vs. society." It would appear to me a more effective tenet if it asked us to direct our climbing efforts to "the ongoing transformation of all societies, including the church."

Thursday, May 3, 2007

Tenet 6. Scripture Alone

Tenet 1. God is.
Tenet 2. God elects every human.
Tenet 3. Every human is response-able (a steward) to God.
Tenet 4. Covenantal Life is for the Common Good.
Tenet 5. Ongoing Transformation of All Societies.
Tenet 6. Scripture alone, Grace alone, Faith alone.

Per Wikipedia: "Sola scriptura (Latin ablative, 'by scripture alone') is the assertion that the Bible as God's written word is self-authenticating, clear (perspicuous) to the rational reader, its own interpreter ('Scripture interprets Scripture'), and sufficient of itself to be the only source of Christian doctrine. Sola scriptura was a foundational doctrinal principle of the Protestant Reformation held by the reformer Martin Luther and is a definitive principle of Protestants today. (see Five solas)"

Per Wikipedia: "Sola scriptura may be contrasted with Roman Catholic and Eastern Orthodox teaching, in which the Bible must be interpreted by church teaching, by considering the Bible in the context of Sacred Tradition."

How can this rigid tenet help me in my climb?

How does one explain in a few sentences something as serious as the fact that one questions attributing essential tenet stature to the Bible (God's written word), to Scripture alone, with its myths, metaphors and contradictions? The answer is, of course, "One cannot."

But, then, how can "Scripture alone" explain, and be, the sole contact by Cosmic God with the intellect and the pinch of spirit within untold generations of billions of humans, who lived prior to, or unaware of, the Scriptures. The answer is, of course, "One cannot."

It is my assumption that some individuals or a group ahead of me experienced this same dilemma and took away the "aloneness" of Scripture by including Grace and Faith in the tenet.

Thus Cosmic God of the Universe extends Grace beyond merely being the Scriptural God of the Bible Verse and our Faith is not restricted to idolizing the Bible.

Friday, May11, 2007

Tenet 7. The Incarnation

Tenet 1. God is.
Tenet 2. God elects every human.
Tenet 3. Every human is response-able (a steward) to God.
Tenet 4. Covenantal Life is for the Common Good.
Tenet 5. Ongoing Transformation of All Societies.
Tenet 6. Scripture Alone, Grace Alone, Faith Alone.

Tenet 7. The Incarnation.

Wikipedia: "The doctrine of the Incarnation of Christ is central to the traditional Christian faith as held by the Roman Catholic Church, the Eastern Orthodox Church, and most Protestants. In the Incarnation, the divine nature of the Son was perfectly united with human nature in one divine Person, truly God and truly man. This doctrine is specifically referenced in the Bible. It is known as hypostatic union.

The final definitions of the incarnation and the nature of Jesus were made by the early Church at the Council of Ephesus, the Council of Chalcedon and the First Council of Nicaea. These councils declared that Jesus was both fully God, begotten from the Father; and fully man, taking His flesh and human nature from the Virgin Mary. These two natures, human and divine, were hypostatically united into the one personhood of Jesus Christ."

Does being specifically referenced in the Bible (John 1:14 and Colossians 2:9) make a statement true? If true why were months of discussions at the Council of Ephesus, the Council of Chalcedon and the First Council of Nicaea necessary?

`What if John or Paul had said the following? "All humans are response-able. Jesus is the personification of ultimate response-ableness."

What if the Council of Ephesus, the Council of Chalcedon and the First Council of Nicaea, after months of discussion had decided, "Yes, all humans are reponse-able to the Cosmic God that, through an infusion which we can't comprehend, places a pinch of Cosmic Spirit into each human. Humans apply their individual pinches of Spirit to life with varying results. At a given moment in history, a man named Jesus used his pinch in such manner that his life of response-ableness became the ultimate model for human kind. This once only model is of such a powerful, universal nature that the human, being a response-able steward, does not require a mythological, once only model of, truly God/truly man through a process labeled hypostasis."

I find the ultimately response-able, steward-Jesus tenet to be a much more functional tenet to follow upslope than the hypostatically, truly man/truly God, incarnated Jesus doctrine which has come to be the central orthodoxy of the Christian belief.

Does the church have the Faith through Grace to study further both concepts?

Sunday, May 13, 2007

Tenet 8. The Trinity

Tenet 1. God is.
Tenet 2. God elects every human.
Tenet 3. Every human is response-able (a steward) to God.
Tenet 4. Covenantal Life is for the Common Good.
Tenet 5. Ongoing Transformation of Societies.
Tenet 6. Scripture Alone, Grace Alone, Faith Alone.
Tenet 7. The Incarnation.
Tenet 8. The Trinity.

Wikipedia: "In Christianity, the doctrine of the Trinity states that God is one being who exists, simultaneously and eternally, as a mutual indwelling of three persons: the Father, the Son (incarnate as Jesus of Nazareth), and the Holy Spirit. Since the 4th century, in both Eastern and Western Christianity, this doctrine has been stated as "one God in three persons," all three of whom, as distinct and co-eternal persons, are of one indivisible Divine essence, a simple being. Supporting the doctrine of the Trinity is known as Trinitarianism. The majority of Christians are Trinitarian, and regard belief in the Trinity as a test of orthodoxy."

Since the genesis of intellect the human has determined life, and all that is, as comprised of a tripartite existence.

creation - the universe, the Earth, nature and all life require a Creator (Maker).

sustentation - the heavens, suns, stars, all life, require a Sustainer (Supporter).

redemption - all things physical and spiritual require a Redeemer (Healer).

Even when one God was finally determined to be a superior deity to many gods, the One God was thought to display these three sets of Characteristics (Persons).

How obvious, then, the following conclusion

... The Creator/Maker is God as the One Father. The Supporter/ Sustainer is God as the Incarnate Son. The Redeemer/ Healer is God as a Holy Spirit.

It took three to four centuries and multiple Councils for this "One God in three persons" to be accepted. Once accepted it took even more time for the Trinity to become a test of orthodoxy.

If God created all that is in six days (as some believe), why did the concept of the Trinity take 2,400 years to evolve and become a tenet?

Why was it four hundred years following the birth of the Son before multiple Councils developed the Trinitarian doctrine?

I find the individual titles Incomprehensible, Cosmic God, Ultimately Response-Able, Steward Jesus and Indescribable, Spiritual Essence to be more descriptive than a tripartite, anthropomorphic phrase, The Trinity, from prolonged councils of the Fourth Century. ... Could this be reason for more study?

Thursday, May 17, 2007

Redux

With my March 15, 2007 blog titled "Amazing" I contemplated my journey up Dr. Martin Luther King's metaphorical mountain from which he hoped to see the promised land. Has he now seen the promised land? Our intellect cannot tell us. Does God's Amazing

Grace acting through our response-able faith give us the hope that Dr. King has and that someday we may?

We humans add rules and requirements to our climb. Over the centuries we have developed these rules and requirements within our religious systems to describe and define our relationship with God. Because these rules define and authenticate this awesome relationship we give them special names, doctrines and tenets.

As humans have espoused, then subscribed to and supported these doctrines and tenets, oral and written accounts of their applications have retroactively attributed the primary genesis of such doctrines to God and their secondary distribution to humans.

If we subscribe to and support these doctrines and tenets in a manner approved by various human traditions, our beliefs are termed orthodox (right and true, established and approved). If we question or doubt these doctrines and tenets, we risk being labeled unorthodox or apostate by some who claim orthodoxy.

Our response-able, metaphysical faiths want to assume that God, through Amazing Grace, will preserve our pinches of spirit in a promised land at the end of our climb. This is the one essential tenet held by a vast majority of humans of all religions.

But - many within and without the church have come to the point of critical dilemma. The Christian Church over the centuries has evolved many, many tenets and doctrines that point toward and elaborate on this primary or basic tenet. Currently within the Presbyterian Church with its several branches, and the Christian Church with its innumerable bodies, the multiplicity of doctrines and rules has become as a plethora to the life blood of these many churches and church bodies.

Many of us within the Presbyterian Church USA sit by its bedside trying this infusion and that as it struggles to overcome a blockage in first this part and then the other caused by various coagulating, ecclesial systems, each claiming to be the true orthodoxy which alone can restore and sustain the church's viability.

Can the church be saved by discussions using scriptures as projectiles and hurling tenets as missiles? Do these intense confrontations, which continue to fail, exemplify a fullness of love or the emptiness of insanity?

Must the church go on life support before we realize that it is dying?

Wednesday, May 23, 2007

Redux Revisited

Or as Yogi Berra said - "Deja vu all over again."

"Can the church be saved by discussions using scriptures as projectiles and hurling tenets as missiles? Do these intense confrontations, which continue to fail, exemplify a fullness of love or the emptiness of insanity?

Must the church go on life support before we realize that it is dying?"

These were the final words of my May 16, 2007 blog titled "Redux." Had I thought these words through thoroughly before I released them in a blog?

I had indeed. Here follows a compression of my reasoning behind the quote repeated above.

Parts of the church, not the entire church but sizable portions of it, are involved in direct, intense confrontations. Unfortunately all portions of the Presbyterian Church USA not involved directly are involved vicariously, since the PCUSA is a constitutional body.

All one has to do is read the ecclesial positions, agendas, doctrinal proclamations and oppositional defamations by the polarized constituents to realize that the PCUSA is being torn by a struggle to the death. Both sides claim to portray the will of God and each side claims to exemplify a fullness of love because they assert that beyond the conflict they have love for the other.

I would venture that the very nature of the conflict cannot exemplify any such fullness of love but demonstrates the emptiness of insanity. Not the primary definition of being insane - "a deep organic insanity, mental illness or madness," but one of the secondary definitions - "the shallow behavioral insanity of being extremely foolish, irrational and illogical."

Einstein – "One is insane, when one keeps on doing what one has been doing but continues to expect different results."

Any of us who claim to be members of the body of Christ (either the incarnate human/divine Jesus or the ultimately response-able steward Jesus) who demonstrate hate, or pity, for brothers and sisters in Christ to the point that "our orthodoxy" denies others salvation -- have forsaken love and chosen emptiness.

Perhaps the fullness of love will come by 2400 CE when all parties to the current conflict have opened their hearts and minds to at least 400 years (eg. Nicaea, Ephesus, Chalcedon) of Grace Filled Councils with this question as their agenda:

"Is the Cosmic Force the Incomprehensible God of the Universe or the Doctrinal God of the Bible Verse?"

Wednesday, May 30, 2007

Redux Revisited Again

The May 17, 2007 blog titled "Redux" contained a question I have failed to answer: "Must the church go on life support before we realize that it is dying?" Hence the "Revisited Again" title of this blog.

In the May 17, 2007 blog I started to answer the question as follows:

"All one has to do is read the ecclesial positions, agendas, doctrinal proclamations and oppositional defamations by the polarized constituents to realize that the PCUSA is being torn by a struggle to the death."

Bishop John Shelby Spong approaches the dilemma on a much broader scope and expands on the topic in a book titled: "Why Christianity Must Change or Die."

In this blog let's just discuss briefly the four areas in my sentence above.

a. ecclesial (ecclesiastical) positions: over old and new centuries segments of the church have developed traditions and practices which have become the very blood and breath within that segment's concept of the church. Some opine that the church might just as well die as give up these positions. Thus a struggle to the death.

b. agendas: I realize that agenda is a secular word which merely resembles what the church calls its mission. At present various and sundry segments of the church are not behaving as if they have a mission. They are willing to struggle to the death over agendas.

c. doctrinal proclamations: To me (and I do not have any intent of proclaiming this for others) the Judeo-Christian Bible conveys four precepts - Myth, Reality, A Set of Laws, and Good News. We struggle to the death over too many doctrines that derive from a fullness of Myth and Law and then proclaim an emptiness of Reality and Good News.

d. oppositional defamations: When, within religious confrontations, any Position A is willing to deny fellow humans life, present or eternal, because they do not follow orthodoxy as defined by Position A, the struggle simply must not be permitted unto the death.

The struggle must be what dies for if it continues there can be no Reality or Good News.

Wednesday, June 06, 2007

Incomprehensible or Doctrinal?

"Is the Incomprehensible God of the Universe the Cosmic Force or is the Doctrinal God of the Bible Verse the Cosmic Force?"

On March 27, 2007 the blog was titled "Preparing for the Climb." In the intervening weeks the blogs have presented some of the trails up my mountain and some of the tools essential to the climb up all our mountains toward a view of the Promised Land.

I am still climbing but I am becoming curious about what I can expect to view when I reach the top. Paul Tillich tells me that the Ground of All Being will spread before me. Martin Buber promises I - Thou relationships. A recent book by Gene Marshall stresses that I will see and hear "The Call of the Awe." (Search Google for: "Gene Marshall - Realistic Living.")

When I started my chronological climb many decades ago I believed (no, I KNEW) God to be the anthropomorphic God-Person who would take my soul - "If I should die before I wake." (With apologies to the anecdote wherein Karl Barth supposedly claimed this prayer to be the summation of his theology.)

As I have climbed the mountain, over these years, I have gradually transitioned to the faith that God is a Cosmic Force "luring the Earthen histories upslope" (Rolston). Although I cannot comprehend this Force, I have faith that this Cosmic Force is God luring me up the mountain.

My transition is gradually, irresistibly moving me from a dependency on doctrinal beliefs, structured by humans, and from a dependancy on Bible verses, interpreted (literally or otherwise) by humans, to a broader, ahistorical, beyond Biblical, concept of God:

"The divine spirit is the giver of life, pervasively present over the millennia. God is the atmosphere of possibilities, the metaphysical environment, in, with, and under first the natural and later also the cultural environment, luring the Earthen histories upslope." (To complete the Rolston quote.)

The Judeo-Christian Bible, and those doctrines which derive from it, are historical and mythical portions of the Earthen histories within God's atmosphere of possibilities. Through my lifelong Christian orientation much of my faith flows naturally from this portion of God's atmosphere.

But now many of us within the church, and many who choose to remain outside the church, view with alarm the church's internal, confrontational turmoil which rages in the name of tenets, doctrines, morals, agendas, orthodoxies. . . . even worse - rages under the name of pseudo theology.

Thus it is difficult for many who search for God to base their faith in the Doctrinal God of the Bible Verse when they sense that the atmosphere of possibilities is primarily comprised of the Incomprehensible God of the Universe.

In his book, "The Pale Blue Dot" Carl Sagan presents this summary statement:

"A religion, old or new, that stressed the magnificence of the Universe as revealed by modern science might be able to draw forth reserves of reverence and awe hardly tapped by conventional faiths. Sooner or later such a religion will emerge."

Such a religion will not, can not, emerge from the current struggle within the PCUSA. Both sides to this struggle claim responsibility to and for tenets, doctrines, morals, agendas and orthodoxies of divergent natures and rigidities instead of pursuing the basic mission - seeking to be response-able to God.

Being response-able to God must be reviewed and reconstituted in human minds through unpredictable years of Grace filled study and change so that it can demonstrate reverence and awe for the Incomprehensible God of the Universe as opposed to dependency on contestable doctrines and orthodoxies.

The question answered: The Incomprehensible God of the Universe will one day be recognized as the Cosmic Force.

Tuesday, June 12, 2007

How?

How will the current turmoil which rages within the PCUSA (Presbyterian Church in the USA) be soothed and solved?

The local Presbyterian Church (USA) which I have attended for 60 years installed new, stained glass, sanctuary windows in 1956. Each of the 10 windows (five to a side) carried an insert denoting a Christian symbol e.g. the Bible, a cross, a dove, a ship. The front window on the left of the sanctuary had an insert depicting a castle on a rock with the words "A Mighty Fortess" worked into the lower arc of the circle surrounding the symbol. It was not until many years after the installation that someone noticed that the key word in the symbol had been misspelled FORTESS instead of FORTRESS.

What to do?

It would require much labor and expense to remove the window and correct the insert. It had remained unnoticed for many years. Why initiate change or the potential for turmoil over change?

And so the error simply remains uncorrected and unmentioned.

But. This misspelling is a miniscule example of how a congregation can manage what to some might appear to be the need for concern and change.

Currently congregations in the PCUSA and other branches of the Christian Church, even Christianity in toto, face conflicts immeasurably more serious and deadly than misspelled words.

Conflicts abound over: tenets, doctrines, orthodoxies, infallibility of the Bible, salvation, ordination standards, sexual orientation, definitions of sin, and on and on.

Can the Christian Church permit these conflicts to remain uncorrected and unmentioned?

No. These conflicts are so serious and deadly that it appears entirely logical for author John Shelby Spong to title a book: "Why Christianity Must Change or Die."

The church changed, even while developing, through the centuries until the 16th Century when it underwent a cataclysmic split coincidental with a massive reformation. The fact that it did not die then is no promise that it will not die from a next cataclysm.

So. It does not appear safe to assume that the Christian Religion will split itself (into a duo), or prune itself (into an uno), so accurately that whatever evolves will be sufficient unto Doctrinal God of the Bible Verse until the end of time. It obviously didn't work the last time around.

A group as dedicated as the Presbyterian Task Force on Peace, Unity, and Purity could not develop any definitive directives that were acceptable to all sides. The Task Force could say unanimously at the end that those within the group had come to respect one another. Could they share that "how to" with the church? Would that help?

Therefore. What if we all put our hearts and our minds together, instead of our spleens and our biliousness, and developed some common sense materials on how to respect one another so that we can discuss: tenets, doctrines, orthodoxies, infallibility of the Bible, salvation, ordination standards, sexual orientation, definitions of sin, etc., without assuming that ideas which might differ from ours are: too orthodox, too unorthodox, too biblical, too unbiblical, too flexible, too rigid, too this or too that.

What say? What if? We study HOW to solve current conflicts and prevent future ones.

The next blog will propose the WHO for the process. Perhaps that can make the HOW easier?

Thursday, June 21, 2007

Who?

WHO will soothe and solve the turmoil that rages within the Presbyterian Church (USA)?

From the April 20, 2007 blog about Stewardship as a tenet - this statement:

. . . " stewardship to God is the ultimate role for humans as they seek meaning for life. What about worship? How better to worship God than to protect God's Earth and Cosmos? What about fellowship? How better to commune with God than to commune with our fellow stewards?"

Who in the Presbyterian Church seeks meaning for life? All the members of the Presbyterian Church should seek meaning for life. All whose membership and priesthood are in a congregation and all whose membership and priesthood are in a presbytery, the laity and the clergy -- should seek meaning for life.

The very existence of this turmoil is counter to the meaning for life.

How many sides are there to the turmoil? How many angels can dance on the head of a pin?

So -- WHO? can solve the turmoil? All of us, of course - clergy and laity who comprise the total of the many sides to, and positions on, this turmoil within the PCUSA.

This is true but it is utterly naive.

Mark Twain ventured that it had been his experience to meet, "many people who are all for progress. It is change they can't tolerate."

Who will put risk ahead of change? Who will learn to tolerate change? It will have to be us - there are no others.

But it cannot be the old us. All of us in the old us have demonstrated no progress through years of trying to effect change. It cannot be one group of us reconciling with the other us because currently most of us have chosen antithetical positions that posit us intractable.

Position 1. What we believe. This is the mirror image of -

Position 2. What we believe others must believe. This is -

Position 3. Orthodoxy.

Without even trying, by practicing Positions 1 and 2, we arrive at Position 3 which we call orthodoxy.

What is orthodoxy? Positions 1 and 2 define it. Position 3 names it.

Does orthodoxy derive from religion or does religion derive from orthodoxy?

Does God reveal orthodoxy? Why, then, does the Doctrinal God of the Bible Verse reveal so many contradictory orthodoxies to so many?

Does the Incomprehensible God of the Universe reveal incomprehensible orthodoxies .... or lure us upslope to comprehension?

As I review my blogs, from February 5, 2007 ("Tenets") forward, I affirm their premise to be that the Church must change. Currently I find that many of my peers (laity and clergy) in the church and many of my peers who should be, but are not in the church, concur with that premise.

WHO? can soothe and solve the turmoil that rages within the Presbyterian Church (USA)? (and in the broader Church?)

Is there hope?

WHO? will project beyond Positions 1, 2, and 3 to a new Comprehension that can change the Church so that it does not die?

Yes, there is hope -- for the Church to be flexible and vital, not rigid and dead.

Monday, July 16, 2007

Why?

Q. Why should the Church change?

A. The Church must change to utilize the expanding and evolving knowledge of the universe within the expanding and evolving of humans' ability to be response-able to the Incomprehensible God of the Universe.

Q. Why should present church members, and those who will become members, make the effort to be the agents of this change?

A. Because luring humanity upslope toward the calm atmosphere of the Incomprehensible God of the Universe is the only way to deter humans from creating the current, toxic climate through self-serving definitions of the Doctrinal God of the Bible Verse.

It will not be easy.

Q. Why will it not be easy?

A. Centuries of tradition and teaching have created many specifics: specific personifications of God, convoluted doctrines, ambiguous tenets. It will take energized counter-forces to effect change. We will face personal anguish as we release our grasps on the Doctrinal God and leap into the Incomprehensible Unknown of the Universal God.

This is as nothing compared to the anguish we shall face as the doctrine-based establishment questions change.

Monday, July 23, 2007

When?

When Positive People Say or Do Negative Things.

When Muslims say that the only way to Paradise is to believe in the Prophet Mohammed, or say that the Qur'an is inerrant, are those speakers: orthodox? fundamentalists? radicals? extremists? terrorists?

When Christians say that the only way to Salvation is to believe in Jesus, or say that the Bible is inerrant, are those speakers: orthodox? fundamentalists? radicals? extremists? terrorists?

If humans are to claim potential positivity for the words and acts of any functioning religion, these humans must analyze the potential results and project whether they will be negative failures or positive successes.

Too much of religion fails this test abysmally because humans' intellectual development of doctrinal Gods has not kept pace with the spiritual potential of the species. Do not be dismayed. This is a work in progress and someday religion will discover the Cosmic God of the Universe.

If an Islamic religious institution should release a fatwa authorizing the killing of nonbelievers, or members labeled heretics, is that homicide?

If a Christian religious institution should release a doctrinal statement denying salvation to any who do not accept Jesus, is that spiritcide?

Tuesday, August 14, 2007

Book Verse vs. Universe

As I reviewed the July 23, 2007 blog, prior to preparing today's, I find a thought that I believe should be expanded and phrased to read like this:

"The potential of humans to relate spiritually to the Incomprehensible God of the Universe has not kept pace with human intellects as they have fabricated Doctrinal Gods of the Book Verse. Such a relationship with the Cosmic God will not attain maturity, even in this enlightened era, for several generations - but it will develop."

Book religions are especially susceptible to developing doctrines from verses or ideas within their books. It is when the Incomprehensible God is reduced to a doctrinal god that religions are at risk of fabricating a god owned by that religion.

Attempting to merge all religions into one universal religion is not compatible with most humans' reasoning capabilities. Tribal and cultural imprints would never tolerate such a concept of unity. However, both our seminal and our teleological reasoning assure us that there is a Cosmic God and that each human has a primal spirit that can relate to that God.

When humans find themselves in, or choose, a delimited, religious belief system, too often they also choose to impose a belief change on other humans. That imposition can even behave in belligerent contra-distinction to the more worthy principles of the system from which it devolves.

Does the reader remember the question we asked in the February 5, 2007 blog, "What ails the Church?" It is here that we find ourselves caught up in the current turmoil within the Presbyterian Church USA.

The turmoil is grounded in this: two doctrinal positions extrapolated from the same book have developed differing tenets and belief systems, each having its own concept of God. The inference of each side is that the other position is in error and if only that position would change, healing could occur.

The inference of each side is incorrect. Healing will occur when both sides recognize that their true calling is to be response-able, not to their Doctrinal God of the Book Verse but to the Incomprehensible God of the Universe.

Saturday, August 25, 2007

Real yet Incomprehensible

Here is the summary statement from the August 14, 2007 blog relative to the current status of the turmoil within the Presbyterian Church USA:

"The inference of each side is incorrect. Healing will occur when both sides recognize that their true calling is to be response-able, not to their Doctrinal God of the Book Verse but to the Incomprehensible God of the Universe."

The label "Tower of Babel" (Babel is etymologized by association with the Hebrew verb balal, "to confuse or confound") is as a one pixel blip compared to the mega label "Tower of Assumption" which critics will heap on the statement in the previous paragraph.

Let's look at some of the errors that the statement will be accused of?

1. In religious controversies each side is so God assured that it is correct and the other side is wrong that a third party claiming that both are incorrect has no authenticity whatsoever with Infallible God.
2. With the Infallible Doctrinal God of the Bible Verse there is no neutral. There is only right or wrong because totally infallible means just that.

It was Mark Twain who, lacking conventional theological credentials, made this statement: "Total abstinence is so excellent a thing that it cannot be carried to too great an extent. In my passion for it I even carry it so far as to totally abstain from total abstinence itself."

Could there be a miniscule chance that all those many who abstain from accepting the Bible as totally infallible might coincidentally be other than totally fallible?

3. The critics will ask, "How can the human be response-able to an Incomprehensible God, with no book to define the nature of that God?"

But, how did those who wrote the book come by it? Oh, yes. it was divine revelation. Odd how so many writers were and are left out of the revelation cycle. Stranger still, some of the writings that made it in.

A conclusion - there are just as many sound questions on our side as on the side of those who question our abstention from infallibility. How then can they refute this, "We find the Cosmic God real, yet Incomprehensible."

Tuesday, August 28, 2007

We Disagree

Not only do we disagree within the church, there is disagreement within our nation. Worse, there is disagreement throughout the world. I've tried to capsulize three huge areas of disagreement - religious, national political, geopolitical - into a composite poem.

Then? What can we do ?

Maybe the next several blogs can explore this?

We disagree, he and me.
I say, God is one.
He says God is three.

He says it is apparent
God's Bible is inerrant.
I say that it was human writ,
And all the parts just do not fit.

He says the plan since first creation,
Christ alone leads us to salvation.
I say that makes the gate too narrow,
If God takes care of every sparrow.

To me it was folly, going into Iraq.
His pledge - throw bombs, get roses back.
7 in 10 say, Bring home our troops with quick finesse.
3 say, We can't. The Iraqis've made things such a mess.

He says our country's on the up track.
I say no, that I see it a slippin' back.
I say there's too much global warmin,'
He says that's just more libral yarnin.'

65

We disagree, he and me.
God loves him. God loves me.
That makes us three.

Tuesday, September 18, 2007

Worship

Since my August 28, 2007 blog, the poem about religious, national-political and world-geopolitical disagreements, I've taken a break from blogging and spent my spare time studying what others offer as ways to solve the world's plethora of disagreements.

As I have read or heard the thoughts of various individuals and entities it comes to me that "Mission" is the current, preeminent, descriptive term for solutions to the various dilemmas which humans face. However, this concept of mission is not a generic, human mission, open to all. Rather it is restricted to the religious, to those who claim to understand better than others how to relate to the divine or supernatural. As I explore many examples of this word, mission, I believe missions fit into one of two categories.

Category 1. Those missions through which the human relates to God.

Example a. Worship. I recently read an author who was adamant that worship (as prescribed by the author) can solve all problems.

Category 2. Those missions through which the human relates to humans.

Example a. Evangelism. Another author sees evangelism as the most important solution to all disagreements.

In this blog I would have us consider worship.

Ever, since I can remember, I have worshipped God. Gradually over those years I have exchanged my belief in a comprehensible God of the rigid Bible Verse for belief in an incomprehensible God of the flexible Universe. I now find more truth in transparency than in inerrancy.

Today, in public worship, I have no difficulty worshipping a God different from the one of my heritage. This current God permits me to remain silent in worship when others state that they have just heard Scriptures read as the Word of God. Instead, I heard words of humans who had a reverend relationship with their God in their time and their culture.

This more recent, incomprehensible God does not punish me when I remain silent through much of certain creeds. I no longer comprehend that there is a hell and the incomprehensible God does not send lightning when I refuse to recite in a creed that Christ "descended to hell." In fact I just read the claim that by far the majority of church members no longer believe there is a literal hell. If this claim is true, why do we permit such an idea to compromise and distort our worship experience and our relationship with the supernatural?

One article I read named worship as the most important way for the church to achieve spiritual revival. As I read further into this article's concept of worship, it became apparent that the tone of the worship being extolled was not for spiritual change but for reinforcement of an existing spiritual status quo. This most important worship was not to be a communication with God about supporting all sides in disagreements or transforming all of society. Rather, it was to be an assurance that, if God corrected those of the other side and transformed them, God would merit our all important worship.

It has come to me over years of observing various religions, that the author Caroline Myss has found an apt metaphor when she decries much of religion as a "costume party." I speak only of my own worship, which I know better than that of others, when I discover my worship costume of piety to be periodic dress-up clothes compared to the permanent rags of poverty which too many must endure.

No, I'm afraid worship is not the most important way to achieve spiritual change that solves disagreements.

In the next blog we'll consider evangelism as a solution.

Sunday, September 23, 2007

A Correction

In rereading the September 17, 2007 blog as preparation for writing the next blog, I found a flaw in the next to the last sentence of that blog.

The sentence read, "No, I'm afraid worship is not the most important way to achieve spiritual change which solves disagreements."

The sentence should have been written, "No, I'm afraid worship of the Comprehensible God of the Bible Verse is not the most important way to achieve spiritual change which solves disagreements."

For all these weeks of blogging I have contrasted the Incomprehensible God of the Universe with the Comprehensible God of the Bible Verse. Then the chance to utilize the cognitive value of the statement arises and I blow it.

I do not pretend that the contrastive awareness of a comprehensible God vs. an incomprehensible God is currently unique. It has been around as long as religion. It speaks as a counter claim to religion's original and "ever since" claim that follows:

The first claim is to comprehend God. The second claim is to add as an overlay the comprehension that the first comprehension was a direct revelation from that comprehensible God. This is the perpetual motion of religion. It is in recording suppositions as comprehensions that humans have tried to render God large and comprehensible. It is in refusing to permit God to be beyond comprehension that religions render God small.

Could it be that, in claiming revelation of human suppositions as divinely inspired comprehensions, religions through all of time have maligned God's Grace - and humans' veracity? A wrathful God selecting those to be inmates of a literal hell under the supervision of an evil Satan comes to mind as an example of such distortions.

Do not all religions (PCUSA included) diminish the spiritual stretch of adherents into the incomprehensible supernatural by framing human suppositions as dogmatized comprehensions?

Monday, October 15, 2007

Evangelism

If our primary mission as humans is to relate to God, whether the Comprehensible God of the Bible Verse or the Incomprehensible God of the Universe, we can relate best if we understand God to be love.

If God is love the human in a worship relationship does not enhance or magnify the God that has been love for billions of years prior to the human. Worship is not adulation of God. Worship is not a begging for God's love toward us. Worship is beseeching God to empower us to use love as we relate to other humans and to all of God's nature.

Worship can be defined as asking God to show us how to give love away. Evangelism is that actual giving (sharing). So here we are at evangelism, our secondary mission.

In the Sound of Music, Rodgers and Hammerstein tell us, "The love in your heart wasn't put there to stay, love isn't love 'til you give it away."

Alfred B. Smith (1916-2001) wrote a well-known child's action song:

If you're happy and you know it, clap your hands.
If you're happy and you know it, clap your hands.
If you're happy and you know it,
And you really want to show it,

If you're happy and you know it, clap your hands.

May I transpose Rodgers and Hammerstein's thought to Alfred B. Smith's style?

If you've learned God is love, clap your hands.
If you've learned God is love, clap your hands.
If God is love and you know it,
And you really want to show it,
Pass God's love on to others, clap your hands.

Evangelize, as found in dictionaries, has two very separate and distinct meanings:

    1. Convert or seek to convert someone to Christianity.

or

    2. To preach the Christian Gospel: the church's mission is to evangelize the faith.

    1. Can we convert another person? We can give love away but we have no control over how the recipient uses it. I can not even be sure of my own motivation within the giving. Mark Twain was being realistic, at least for me, when, in "What Is Man," he noted human nature as including:
"That desire which is in us all to better other people's condition by having them think as we think."

    2. Is evangelism exclusively symbiotic with the Christian Gospel, the Christian Faith? Is God's love franchised?

My better judgment would be to end this blog with these questions and give us a respite for serious thought. I believe I will. The assignment for this respite is:

How much of the current conflict within and without the church comes because we cannot comprehend the extent of the

Incomprehensible God's love or grasp how to evangelize (share) that love?

Friday, October 19, 2007

Another Correction

In the most recent blog of October 15, 2007, entitled "Evangelism," I stated:

"If God is love the human in a worship relationship does not enhance or magnify the God that has been love for billions of years prior to the human. Worship is not adulation of God. Worship is not a begging for God's love toward us. Worship is beseeching God to empower us to expand love as we relate to other humans and to all of God's nature."

Very quickly the following comment from a much respected source appeared in my e-mail inbox:

"RE: your October 15 blog. I would agree with nearly all of it, and I think our church is walking a path of loving the Incomprehensible God. The part in which I differ a bit is my belief that we do add something to God (or take away) by how we love and live. The more we are in love the more we are in God and so the more fulfilled God can be. Our choices matter. Also, when I die God loses an infinitely small opportunity to be the ground and receiver of my love, so a new human is born."

My source is right. Here follows my response to this source.

"Of course! I've rolled your belief that we can add something to God around in my mind and come to the conclusion that you are on target. I had fallen into the Biblical supposition that God is comprehensible and unchangeable. Wrong! If that which images God can be fulfilled then God's fulfilling the human adds to God's fulfillment."

Please note that I am not taking this proof statement ('that which images God') from the suppositions within the Bible but from every extinct and extant human's innate pinch of Incomprehensible Love (the pinch of Spirit). These are the same innate suppositions utilized by those who wrote the Bible Verse. Incomprehensible Love is what defines and drives us as human images of Incomprehensible God in the Universe."

Another approach is to understand that the Cosmos is constantly expanding (as confirmed by scientific data and observation) which lends credence to the theological supposition that Incomprehensible Love is also capable of constant expansion.

I'll leave the October 15, 2007 blog standing as is with its error, now followed by this correction. Being wrong periodically and admitting it is a more comfortable state of existence than constantly assuming that one is right and defending it.

Thursday October 25, 2007

Contradictions.

Before the last correction was inserted, this blog series invited the readers to rest and study the following dilemma:

"How much of the current conflict within and without the church comes because we cannot comprehend the extent of the Incomprehensible God's love or grasp how to evangelize (share) that love?"

We have offered for consideration that worship (beseeching God to show us how to share God's love) and evangelism (the actual sharing) are the two most urgent missions of the church and its adherents.

What if . . . our comprehensions of God's love are anthropomorphically skewed?

First let us study for a moment the Comprehensible God of the Bible Verse and the two ultimate Biblical accounts of that God's comprehensible love; the first in the Old Testament and the second in the New Testament.

Ultimate Account 1: The Comprehensible God of the Old Testament Bible Verse is portrayed as saving God's (chosen) people mythically or literally (reader's choice) from slavery into deliverance via the Exodus. This act of saving love came at the price of the death of untold, innocent, first-born Egyptians and the drowning of countless enemy soldiers, guilt or innocence unknown. For centuries many humans have found this God and this peculiar manifestation of God's love comprehensible.

Ultimate Account 2: The Comprehensible God of the New Testament Bible Verse is portrayed as saving (literally and eternally) all who believe, (through a leap of faith) that God planned (permitted?) the death of Jesus (the ultimately response-able human) as the atonement for our self-perpetrated sins. For centuries many humans have found this God and this peculiar manifestation of God's love comprehensible.

Now. Back to our question:

"How much of the current conflict within and without the church comes because we cannot comprehend the extent of the Incomprehensible God's love or grasp how to evangelize (share) that love?"

Could it be that we cannot utilize the love of the Incomprehensible God of the Universe because we have been given by the Bible's writers a faulted comprehension of the love of the Comprehensible God of the Bible Verse?

Wholesale deaths of innocent, first-born Egyptians and the unwarranted death of the ultimately response-able Jesus appear to contradict accounts intended to demonstrate (prove?) that Biblical God is love.

Thursday, November 1, 2007

Contumely

We have reached a point of review.

In the blog of March 29, 2007 I had adopted Martin Luther King's metaphor of climbing the mountain and was preparing to climb. I climbed from March, 2007 for much of the summer through the essential tenets of the Presbyterian Church toward the To-Be-Known-Land. During the climb the writings held fast to the One God but discovered many comprehensions and interpretations of that One God. As examples:

God is the Atmosphere of Possibilities, luring human histories upslope. God is The Awe. The Doctrinal God of the Bible Verse. The Cosmic God of the Universe. The Comprehensible God of the Bible Verse. The Incomprehensible God of the Universe.

In my early years awareness of God was handed to me by my family and my culture. These sources put me primarily in contact with The Doctrinal/Comprehensible God of the Bible Verse. But as I think back to those years there was always present in our three generational Presbyterian household permission to build a belief system note by note into a flexible melody rather than brick by brick into a rigid wall. Thus I have not had to overcome the dilemma that many face as they change their belief systems from rigid and structured to flexible and melodious.

My transition has occurred over many years but my exercise of translating that transition into written form has happened over more recent years. Here I am. I have climbed Martin Luther King's mountain and can see the road to the To-Be-Known Land just ahead. Immediately I see a fork in the road. Do I follow Yogi Berra's advice, "When you come to a fork in the road - take it?"

No, it is not that simple. Especially when the two road signs read:

Road to the Comprehensible God of the Bible Verse.
Road to the Incomprehensible God of the Universe.

Here we are, barely into the To-Be-Known-Land and we find that it is more accurately the Land of Contumely. Secular contumely. No faith contumely, Religious contumely. Interfaith contumely, Intrafaith contumely. On-and-On contumely.

For the next series of blogs I shall explore, and hopefully evaluate, the State of Contumely within the Presbyterian Church (USA) from the perspective of an average Presbyterian lay person. A part of the exploration will be to determine if the present Presbyterian Contumely is Intra-Presbyterian or Inter-Presbyterian.

Stated differently: has schism occurred, is it occurring, will it occur, how far will it go?

Monday November 12, 2007

Contumely and Schism

What do I mean by the State of Contumely within the Presbyterian Church (USA)?

Amazingly, when I go to my computer's dictionary for a definition of the word contumely it is almost as if I had written the definition to serve my specific essayist need on this very occasion, contumely - insolent or insulting language or treatment: the church should not be exposed to gossip and contumely. Origin: late middle language.

The coincidence grows. My e-mail brings me today a news release from the Presbyterian Church in the USA (via PCUSANEWS) which reports that [a specific PCUSA church] "has voted to leave the PCUSA for the Evangelical Presbyterian Church (EPC). The vote of the congregation on Oct. 28 - with less than one-third of its members present - was 422-60."

"'We want to conduct our mission with clarity about the Lordship of Jesus Christ and the authority of Scripture,' said [the pastor], who is a member of the New Wineskins, the group that has led the departure of a number of PC(USA) congregations to the EPC."

"In a letter to members of the congregation posted on the church's Web site before the vote, the session wrote that 'the tolerance of a variety of theological viewpoints has led to theological pluralism in the PC(USA)... After the passage of the PUP (Theological Task Force on Peace, Unity and Purity of the Church) report, discipline is less likely... The PC(USA) is declining and has a limited life span.... Reform has no real chance of success.'"

I quote my previous blog on contumely: "A part of the exploration will be to determine if the present Presbyterian Contumely is Intra-Presbyterian or Inter-Presbyterian. Stated differently: has schism occurred, is it occurring, will it occur, how far will it go?"

When the congregation listed above voted to leave the PCUSA fewer than one-third of the members voted and barely over 29% of the members voted to actually change Presbyterian denominations. This could be classified as Intra-Presbyterian Contumely.

When the Evangelical Presbyterian Church absorbed all members choosing the transfer it became Inter-Presbyterian Contumely.

In this instance one schism has occurred. In other examples available to all of us schisms are occurring and will occur. The truly serious question remains, "how far will it go?"

Monday, November 19, 2007

A Schematic of Schism

Before I structure future blogs to explore "How far will schism go?" I should back up a bit and take a look at why and how schism occurs.

As I reviewed the November 12, 2007 blog, "Contumely and Schism," preparatory to writing today's blog, I realized that the PCUSANEWS #07703 - News Story, 10/31/07 is describing one congregation's (Church A) case history within a potential for Total Schism of the Presbyterian Church USA.

By Total Schism I do not mean splits within congregations over minor, carpet-color issues or even major, pastoral/congregational personality issues. I mean congregations splitting from the denomination over such issues as "theological pluralism," as noted on Church A's Web site.

Based on the news story of this specific church's move, and on similar moves that will continue to occur, such events fit a schematic.

Total Church Schisms - why and how - step by step:

1. The Cause.
Persons, or a person, within a congregation come to a comprehension or doctrinal perception of God that they believe to be at such variance with that of the mother church (the denomination) that the mother must reform or the congregation shall be justified in leaving her.

2. The Process.
In the PCUSA this schismatic process is carried through to an eventual, congregational vote. This process is not necessarily one person/one vote; it is more likely to reflect the relative strengths of power structures and the tactics they employ.

3. The Claims.
Although there are always two or more sides to a schism, all sides claim the same love as their position. Invariably love is displaced by contumely, perhaps in varying amounts on the differing sides.

4. The Reality.

In any active, church schism Murphy's Law: "Whatever can go wrong will go wrong, and at the worst possible time, in the worst possible way," is always more applicable than the Golden Rule.

In the next several blogs we will explore the elements of this schematic, using the Case History of Church A (PCUSANEWS #07703) plus other examples.

Saturday, November 24, 2007

Cause of Schism

1. The Cause. (As listed in the November 19, 2007 blog.)

"Persons (or a person) within a congregation come to a comprehension or doctrinal perception of God which they believe to be at such variance with that of the mother church (the denomination) that the mother must reform or the congregation shall be justified in leaving her."

Although Church A, on its Web site, cites "theological pluralism" as the error of the denomination's ways, these are code words for many current differences with the mother denomination, which the Session of Church A, on the same Web site, described further as. . . "The PC(USA) - which is declining and has a limited life span.... Reform has no real chance of success."

What are some of the comprehensions and doctrinal perceptions of God that put certain pastors, members and congregations at variance with other persons and with their own denomination? I'll list a few but far from all:

The Bible is the inerrant, infallible Word of God.

True God is comprehensible and accessible only to true believers.

The only way to eternal life with this God is through Jesus Christ.

God is love. But, God shares that love disproportionately to true believers and those others of: different belief systems, different religious practices, different vocations, different life styles, different sexual orientations. . .

It is far too simplistic to theorize that schism occurs because some believers know God as Comprehensible and shaped by human doctrinal restrictions while others strive to serve an Incomprehensible God free of human doctrinal restrictions.

However in response to the Session of Church A and its Web site statement: ".... The PC(USA) - which is declining and has a limited life span.... Reform has no real chance of success"... I shall say: "The more members of the PC(USA) who follow the Incomprehensible God of the Universe as contrasted to the Doctrinal God of the Bible Verse the better the chances of PC(USA) reform and success."

Thursday, November 29, 2007

More on Cause.

1. The Cause. "Persons (or a person) within a congregation come(s) to a comprehension or doctrinal perceptions of God which they believe to be at such variance with that of the mother church (the denomination) that the mother must reform or the congregation shall be justified in leaving her."

Who made this decision in Church A? We do not know. It would appear that the Pastor had chosen to join with the call for reforms as voiced by the New Wineskin group. As an extension, did this call then find fertile soil in the Church A Session and enough members of the Church A Congregation to effect a transfer to the "theological unity" of the Evangelical Presbyterian Church as a better fit than the "theological pluralism" of the PCUSA? Again, we can only surmise, we can't know. Who are we to say?

A rhetorical question - Is it ethical for a minister of the word, ordained through vows to certain doctrines within a first denomination, to lead a congregation of that first denomination to a second denomination wherein the minister finds a more personally acceptable set of doctrines?

We hope the reader now realizes that this blogger and many of his peers are not calling for the death of the Christian Church, nor for feeble, tweaking reforms, but for a metamorphosis of those many flawed concepts which stifle the Christian Church in these enlightening times.

Where does the authority for our boldness come from? It comes from wherever Martin Luther's boldness and Martin Luther King's boldness came from - with no claim of any comparable quality or strength. We find that the Doctrinal God of the Bible Verse through vague sectarian mysteries does not challenge us to be as response-able as the Incomprehensible God of the Universe luring us upslope to solve obvious humanitarian needs and realities. e.g. Please contrast the water into wine story for those at an ancient party with a water into milk reality for those in modern poverty.

No one forced this belief system on me, nor shall I force it on any other - by coercion or vote. I have found comfort within the change. The choice was mine. Some may find more comfort in retaining the traditional. Others may feel led to revert from what they call "theological pluralism" to "fundamental unity." These choices are theirs.

The statement, "Christianity must change or die," seems harsh the first time one hears it.

BUT - The more one observes today's Christian Church mired in contumely, the more validity one perceives in the statement.

However, many have come to be more comfortable with the following variant -

Christianity must morph to survive!

Note: Survive is the diametrical opposite of die, but morph is not the diametrical opposite of change. Change could be but a degree of morph.

BUT - How long will metamorphosis take?

Monday, December 3, 2007

How Long?

Christianity must morph to survive. How long will metamorphosis take?

First we need to explore how change can occur. This will be similar in all branches of Christianity but we shall look only at the Presbyterian Church USA.

Pattern 1.

Currently schism is coming to the forefront as the primary modality for change. Congregations split away from the PCUSA to move to another denomination, usually as a reversion to more rigid doctrinal stances in matters of: scriptural authority, way to salvation, sexual orientation, ordination standards, marriage, etc.

Pattern 2.

Tweaking present traditions through constitutional reforms across the entire PCUSA denomination, to achieve expanded diversity and more flexible doctrinal stances, could result in change but not metamorphosis.

Pattern 3.

A gradual morphing of the belief systems of members of the Presbyterian Church USA to comprehend Jesus as the Ultimately Response-Able Human, relieved of metaphysical encumbrances, helping us search for belief in the Incomprehensible God of the Universe in contrast to the Comprehensible God of the Bible Verse.

How Long?

Pattern 1. Schism will never end. By the time today's doctrinal stances have been reestablished for satisfaction in the now, new dilemmas will have arisen to create contumely in the then. Pattern 1. is to no avail.

Pattern 2. Change may postpone the death of Christianity. Only metamorphosis can bring its survival. Pattern 2. is to no avail.

Pattern 3. Metamorphosis will be amazing beyond all concepts of change.

Amazing grace, how sweet the sound
That sav'd a wretch like me!
I once was lost, but now am found,
Was blind, but now I see.*

John Newton wrote this hymn in 1772 as a recall of his conversion while he was on his slave ship, the Greyhound, 24 years earlier in 1748.

In her novel Uncle Tom's Cabin, Harriet Beecher Stowe includes an extra, final verse which may have been taken from another hymn. The additional verse is a part of the hymn in most hymnals today.

When we've been there ten thousand years,
Bright shining as the sun,
We've no less days to sing God's praise

Than when we've first begun.

Per the Amazing Grace formula above perhaps the metamorphosis from the Comprehensible God of the Bible Verse to the Incomprehensible God of the Universe can be amazingly varied - from 24 to 10,000 years?

Pattern 3. IS TO AVAIL - Christianity must morph to survive.

*See: http://en.wikipedia.org/wiki/Amazing_Grace#History

Tuesday, December 11, 2007

Some Statistics

Now back to the fork in the road to the To-Be-Known-Land.

There are the two signs: Road 1 - To the Incomprehensible God of the Universe, Road 2 - To the Comprehensible God of the Bible Verse.

Recall the words of the Session of Church A: "The PC(USA) is declining and has a limited life span.... Reform has no real chance of success."

Many have tried to resist that prediction, but as we struggle the rocky, convoluted trail through the Valley of the Shadow of Death (Christianity must change or die) have we finally been forced to a variant path (Christianity must morph to survive) in order to find hope?

For years many have resisted agreeing with the Session of Church A. But now the realization that contumely within the Doctrinal Kingdom of the Bible Verse is stifling Compassion within the Kindom of the Universe, forces many onto Road 1: To the Incomprehensible God of the Universe.

"The PC(USA) is declining and has a limited life span...."

These are fatalistic words. I went to the PC(USA) web site for information on the decline of the PC(USA).

Here follow direct quotes from the web site:

"Worship attendance as a percent of membership by church size,
Year 2005:

Church Size: 100 or fewer
Attendance as % of membership:
Less than 50% = 20%
50% to 74% = 44%
75% to 99% =24%
100% or more =12%

Church Size: 101-250
Attendance as % of membership:
Less than 50% = 37%
50% to 74% =48%
75% to 99% =11%
100% or more =3%

Church Size: More than 250
Attendance as % of membership:
Less than 50% = 61%
50% to 74% =31%
75% to 99% =6%
100% or more =2%

Note: Totals do not add to 100% due to rounding.

What it means: On a typical Sunday, a larger proportion of the members attend worship in smaller congregations than in larger congregations."

End of direct PC(USA) quote on web site.

We all are well aware that the numbers of PC(USA) churches AND members are declining. It is apparent that those figures are significant.

Are the percentages given in the table above significant? Two questions:

Can we extract directives from these statistics on how the church should morph to survive?

Do these worship attendance statistics correlate with depth or vitality of individual members' belief systems?

Tuesday, December 18, 2007

Worship Redefined

We closed the previous blog with two questions:

1. Can we extract directives from these statistics on how the church should morph to survive?

2. Do these worship attendance statistics correlate with the depth or vitality of individual members' belief systems?

Answers to Question 1.

a. There is the immediate temptation to use the attendance statistics presented to generalize that the smaller the church the better the attendance at worship. However there are so many variables not listed (location, culture, transportation, community economics, competing congregations, on and on) that it is doubtful if generalizations could be valid. Thus any statistics must be used most judiciously.

b. There is the temptation to assume that tweaking the worship format will morph the church.

Here I would ask the reader to return to my blog titled Worship, September 18, 2007. Here follows a segment quoted:

"As I have read or heard the thoughts of various individuals and entities it comes to me that "Mission" is the current, preeminent, descriptive term for solutions to the various dilemmas which humans face. However, this concept of mission is not a generic, human mission, open to all. Rather it is restricted to the religious, to those who claim to understand better than others how to relate to the divine or supernatural. As I explore many examples of this word, mission, I believe missions fit into one of two categories.

Category 1. Those missions through which the human relates to God.
Example a. Worship. I recently read an author who was adamant that worship (as prescribed by the author) can solve all problems.

Category 2. Those missions through which the human relates to humans.
Example a. Evangelism. Another author sees evangelism as the most important solution to all disagreements."

The contradiction I would have us consider is that worship is not the attendance at a specific service once or twice a week. Worship is that mission through which the human relates to God - constantly.
On the basis of that definition it would appear that statistics based on size of congregations and percentages of attendance

at specific services of worship <u>are not values pertinent within the</u> <u>morphing process.</u>

For now this is my answer to Question 1 above. The next blog will deal with Question 2.

Thursday, December 27, 2007

Question 2.

In the previous blog we "sort of" answered Question 1. (about worship and church attendance) with a semi-firm, "No."

We will expand in this blog the answer that, basically, the morphing of Christianity will not occur in response to the analyses of sundry quantitative statistics.

Question 2, repeated: Do these worship attendance statistics correlate with the depth or vitality of individual members' belief systems?

Let's do a bit of review before we answer.

To expand a thought from the October 15, 2007 blog:

Worship is more than mere adulation of God. Worship is not a persistent begging for God's love toward us. Worship is beseeching God to empower us to reflect love as we relate to all other humans and all of God's nature.

Simply put, worship is asking God to use us to give love away. Evangelism is that actual giving (sharing). Worship, our relationship to God, is our first mission. Evangelism, our relationship to humanity, is our second mission.

If we accept this theorem, our God related belief systems are to reflect, and to be, love as we relate to all humans as peers, yes, and as fellow children of God. A qualification: Do we share our beliefs with others because we love them or because we think that if they believe as we do they will be more lovable?

In this light, I refer the reader one more time to the October 15, 2007 blog:

"Mark Twain was being realistic, at least for me, when, in 'What Is Man,' he noted human nature as including: 'That desire which is in us all to better other people's condition by having them think as we think.'"

Twain's statement will be seen by some as sarcasm with a humorous twist, but I see it as defining a trait I struggle to eliminate from my personal human nature.

Statistics can be utilized in changing the forms of institutions but have minimal value in morphing the behavior of humans and hence the functioning of those human institutions.

For many years statistics have revealed the decline of mainstream protestant denominations. Has study of these statistics reversed the decline? The answer is, "No."

Again, do the belief systems of members in small churches have greater depth or vitality than the belief systems of members in large churches because of better attendance at worship services in the smaller churches?

No.

How has it come that Christianity is considered by so many adherents as being other than a human institution while all other religions and secularism are so disconnected from initiation by, or relation to, the supernatural?

Will analyses of statistics morph Christianity?

No.

Why must Christianity morph now to survive (avoid death) later? How much later will statistics on climate change prove deadly? The answers are, "Later is now."

Christianity will morph (and not die) when its worshipping and evangelizing adherents as individuals redirect their personal belief systems from the Comprehensible God of the Bible Verse to the Incomprehensible God of the Universe. This is a current way of stating what one of our nation's founding fathers, John Adams stated early on as follows:

"The question before the human race is, whether the God of nature shall govern the world by His own laws, or whether priests and kings shall rule it by fictitious miracles?"

Many who have left the church and many others, who have not left the church but realize that Christianity must morph to survive, are finding the will to speak of their emerging, changing belief systems. How do the rest of us find the will to listen?

Saturday, December 29, 2007

Paralysis of Analysis

Will analyses of sundry "church" statistics morph Christianity? No.

My December 27 , 2007 blog was intended to clinch the premise that the analysis of statistics is not the basis of a working model for morphing Christianity and hence the church. As I review my notes for preparing that blog I discover that I left out the clincher.

I was going to misquote Jesse Jackson as the originator of the convincing phrase "analysis paralysis." This couplet can emasculate tons of statistics.

When I fed "analysis paralysis - Jesse Jackson" into Google, the Wikipedia answer comes back that this is an informal phrase which is often phrased as "paralysis by analysis." But Wikipedia did not attribute it to Jesse Jackson. Further digging gave me the following address:

http://www.onmilwaukee.com/buzz/articles/mlk.html

and the following article:

OnMilwaukee.com   http://www.onmilwaukee.com/buzz/articles/mlk.html

Milwaukee's Daily Magazine Friday, Dec. 28, 2007
In Milwaukee Buzz:
King's visits to Milwaukee left permanent mark
By OnMilwaukee.com Staff Writers
Published Jan. 15, 2007 at 5:02 a.m.

In his lifetime, Dr. Martin Luther King was known for his splendid oratorical abilities and, especially, his remarkable speeches about racism, equality and other issues vital to the civil rights movement. Many of these orations have, rightfully, become famous and oft-quoted.

Dr. King spoke in Milwaukee on a couple occasions. His first speech here was delivered on Aug. 14, 1956. Neither the morning Sentinel or the afternoon Journal ran anything about this visit.

When he returned on Jan. 27, 1964, for a standing-room-only event at the Milwaukee Auditorium, both papers finally took notice. At the Auditorium Dr. King spoke to 6,300 Milwaukeeans for about 40 minutes. Here are some of the highlights:

- He encouraged people to erase two myths: "Only time can solve the problems of racial integration" and "Civil rights legislation is not important."
- "It may be true that you cannot legislate morality but behavior can be regulated."
- "Law cannot change the heart, but it can restrain the heartless."

- "Time is neutral. It can be used either constructively or destructively ... We must help time and we must realize that the time is always right to do right."
- "We have argued and discussed civil rights enough." He cautioned against getting "bogged down in the PARALYSIS OF ANALYSIS." (caps are mine, E.DeJ.)
- "It takes a strong person to be nonviolent. It has a way of disarming the opposition. He doesn't know what to do. He doesn't know how to handle it."
- "We will be able to hew out of the mountain of despair the stone of hope."

So there we have it. On January 27, 1964 Martin Luther King, Jr. dropped us the phrase that can be a practical deterrent when we are tempted to solve by statistics.

Perhaps it should be said that statistics can be informative but not necessarily reformative. Let's move on.

I've hinted at some things that could morph Christianity and some things that won't. Who am I to be so bold? I figure I've played the role of layperson long enough to be about as average as one can get. In the next blog I'll explore my apologetic (noun) for my series of blogs.

Monday, January 07, 2008

An Apologetic

apologetic (noun) a reasoned argument or writing in justification of something, typically a theory or religious doctrine.

It is January 1, 2008. What better day than January 1 to explore an apologetic for my evolving belief system as promised in my December 29, 2007 blog.

First - permit me to explore the fact that my belief system is not entirely evolutionary and changed but contains innumerable elements of tradition.

Here follows one tiny example:

On this January 1, 2008 my first act of written communication with history was to dig out of my desk a nondescript bundle of paper scraps held by a large paper clip. They were of various sizes, colors and shapes. The only commonalty within the scraps was that each scrap contained one or several inscriptions; January 1, (the year) and the full name of Edgar Kenneth DeJean in his long hand and the same date plus the signature of Elinor Warren DeJean in her long hand. This tradition was one I learned from my grandmother Edith McClellan Wiggs (married to Edgar E. Wiggs). I would have started it about January 1, 1929; as soon as I could pen my name. Only since 1978 have I saved the scraps, but there they are clipped together in the desk.

Beyond family tradition is this a signed promise for good behavior in the new year or a protective superstition for what the new year holds? Is this dated and signed scrap of paper a talisman for safety in the unknown?

Is this a contract with the Comprehensible God of the New Year?

Our lives are combinations of holding fast to traditions while grasping for new realities. The metaphor that explains this belief process to me best is the gradually evolving transition of my belief system away from the Comprehensible God of the Bible Verse to the Incomprehensible God of the Universe.

At this point I find it persuasive to repeat the John Adams quote which appeared in the December 27, 2007 blog:

"The question before the human race is, whether the God of nature shall govern the world by His own laws, or whether priests and kings shall rule it by fictitious miracles?"

How can a very ordinary person, in a series of essays (when posted on the internet they are called blogs), explain a metaphor that would morph a four thousand year old Judeo-Christian, religion?

I've listed many changes that could be positives in morphing Christianity and some ideas that would be negatives. Who am I to be so bold? As I see it, I've played the role of very ordinary person long enough to be about as average as one can get. Furthermore, to encourage me in my eccentricity as I survive more and more years in society and in the church, I find more and more persons who believe as I do. Those who deem us apostate will label us the church's problem. Though the thought of the resistance that will meet our prophetic stance appalls us, we take hope from the fact that it is no longer popular to burn so-called heretics at the stake.

P.S. It is January 7 and in keeping with my pattern I have pondered these thoughts for about a week before posting them. I've given them serious thought and finally, in that rather haughty phrase of the current, presidential campaign era language:

"I approve this message."

Saturday, January 19, 2008

Application

How does one dare to present in print his/her apologetic on a controversial subject?

One can fantasize that the apologetic is so accurate that the world will beat a path to its acceptance. Or one can recognize that it is so radical that the current world will beat it into nonexistence. I find myself somewhere between fantasy and recognition.

Next then, how does one transfer an apologetic from print to application?

In a recent conversation with a Presbyterian pastor he ventured the possibility that the Presbyterian Church, "as we know it today" (his modifier), may not exist in twenty-five years. Even in my most pessimistic moments I hold that those who will morph Christianity have many more years than twenty-five available for the morphing.

When I am saddened by how much dysfunction the Judeo/Christian religion has experienced over its 4,000 years...

I wonder how much dysfunction the church can tolerate, or withstand...

Or - when I honor the wonders that this religion has accomplished in spite of dysfunction...

I glory to imagine what awesome miracles humans could have worked if they had honored the laws of the God of Nature instead of dishonoring each other over pseudo doctrines and fictitious miracles of priests and kings (John Adams' quote expanded)....

How can the masses of believers who, weary of the dysfunctions of priests and kings, now search out the laws of the God of Nature and coalesce to be that morphing force which brings survival to Christianity?

In a previous blog I found us at the fork where we may continue on the road to the Comprehensible God of the Bible Verse or take a leap of faith onto the road to the Incomprehensible God of the Universe, John Adams' God of Nature.

A respected peer, who sees what is but discerns what could be, e-mailed me recently:

"As for the morphing of the church, and your designation of the God of the Universe versus the God of the bible verse ... time will tell where history takes us, and I doubt either you or I will be around to see what results are right now taking root in the world of religion, and how religion and secular views clash or compromise in local, national and international venues. However, I appreciate your thoughts and congratulate you for working on reforming/morphing the church. Can a caterpillar know what the butterfly will be? Keep squirming against the edges of hope and your efforts may help the butterfly to be free!"

In light of this perspective - How to Apply My Apologetic:

I am going to squirm against the edges of hope and present my apologetic for morphing the church through a set of safe travel instructions for the Road to the Incomprehensible God of the Universe.

No doctrines, tenets, demands, commandments, none of these, just some sensible rules for the road . . .

Friday, January 25, 2008

Road Rules

A Travelers Advisory:

Travelers on the road to the Comprehensible God of the Bible Verse are at risk because those who travel it may come to believe that this is the only road to God.

What about the road to the Incomprehensible God of the Universe? There are rules FOR this road in keeping with laws that hold the physical and metaphysical universe together. Rules FOR the road apply to the road itself and its purpose. (In addition there are rules OF this road that apply as directives to its human travelers. We shall explore those directives later.)

Comprehensible humans travel both real and metaphorical roads.

After many years the voice of the speaker for my high school baccalaureate sometimes rattles around in my brain when I face a negative situation. In his booming voice he warned us, and still reminds me: "On the road of life there will be hills ahead."

He may have told us that there would be the pleasures of level ground and the joys of coasting downslope. If he did it went right past my mortarboard.

He certainly did not convey to our class the words of Holmes Rolston, III which I have quoted previously:

"God is the atmosphere of possibilities, the metaphysical environment, in, with, and under first the natural and later also the cultural environment, luring the Earthen histories upslope."

At the moment of my high school baccalaureate I was on the road to the Comprehensible God of the Bible Verse and it is doubtful that I could have grasped the fact that -- "God as the atmosphere of possibilities" was "luring me upslope."

However, it would have been helpful if I could have carried the good news all these years that, "God lures us upslope," as opposed to the dirge that "there will be hills ahead."

It won't be easy:

It won't be simple or easy to search out comprehensible rules from the Laws of the Incomprehensible God of the Universe, but our search will be of no value if we permit our results to match the pseudo doctrines and fictitious miracles of priests and kings.

Here goes:

Rules FOR the Road to the Incomprehensible God of the Universe:

#1 of 3. This road is open to ALL who breathe. The Incomprehensible God of the Universe is the atmosphere of possibilities.

Wednesday, January 30, 2008

Rule 1 FOR the Road

Rule 1. This road is open to ALL who breathe. The Incomprehensible God of the Universe is the atmosphere of possibilities.

Of what value to the Incomprehensible God of the Universe would humans be if there is no road, no connectedness? Of what value is an Incomprehensible God to humans if there is no connectedness?

It is when the human tries to define God and make God comprehensible through mythos, amplified stories, fictitious miracles and illusory revelations that this awesome, mutual connectedness suffers anthropomorphic distortions and diminutions.

It is when these distortions are owned by, or own, specific cultures or religions that these cultures and religions claim to know, and be, the only way to connectedness. They lay claim to the road and other travelers are denied access.

Because God is God of the physical and metaphysical Universe; God establishes the road for connectedness, thus universal access to the road is first a cosmic opportunity, then a human awareness.

When Rule #1 FOR the Road states that the Road is open to all, it is inferred that all who travel it are subject to the same Rules OF the Road. (Rules OF the Road will be explored later.)

Tuesday, February 5, 2008

Rule 2 FOR the Road

Rule 1. This road is open to ALL who breathe. The Incomprehensible God of the Universe is the atmosphere of possibilities.

Rule 2. The primary mission FOR the road is the mutual God-human/ human-God relationship.

Human understanding of, and connectedness with, the Universe expands within nanosecond increments. This is good.

Human understanding of, and connectedness with, God remains immutable within millennial increments. Is this good?

Why, of course, the Universe is physical and its static and kinetic secrets can be measured.

But, of course, God is metaphysical and hence God's secrets are unmeasurable.

So what do humans do? Why, of course, they measure God and God's secrets.

They reveal these measurements as laws, commandments, doctrines, miracles, etc. - stamp them with an "R" for Revelation, and publish them as sacred scrolls, books, letters and, more recently, as blogs.

In a previous blog I proposed that the human has two missions. the first is to be response-able to God. This relationship is the primary reason FOR the road to mutual God/human connectedness that is available to ALL humans. (This is the justification for Rules 1. and 2.)

Rule 1. This road is open to ALL who breathe. The Incomprehensible God of the Universe is the atmosphere of possibilities.

Rule 2. The primary mission FOR the road is mutual God-human/human-God relationship.

The second universal mission of the human is to be responsible to his/her fellow humans. "The love in our hearts wasn't put there to stay - Love isn't love 'til we give it away." This relationship is the secondary reason FOR the road which also serves to bring us to the human/human connectedness essential to ALL humans.

Rule 3 of 3. The secondary mission FOR the road is universal human-human relationships.

Tuesday, February 12, 2008

Rule 3 FOR the Road

Rule 1. This road is open to ALL who breathe. The Incomprehensible God of the Universe is the atmosphere of possibilities.

Rule 2. The primary mission FOR the road is mutual God-human/human-God relationships.

Rule 3. The secondary mission FOR the road is universal human/ human relationships.

Oops!

Sometimes ranking and prioritizing give results that range from confusing to conflictual. This is obvious when we declare the relationship of humans with God to be primary and the relationship of humans with humans to be secondary. But it now occurs to me.... There is a lesson here for me that I would offer for the reader's consideration:

In some long ago moment I heard the rather blunt maxim, "Wise men change their minds, fools never."

I claim neither title, fool nor wise, but I have experienced the benefits that can come from changing one's mind.

May I eliminate ranking and prioritization by condensing the wordings of Rules 2 and 3 to one rule, number 2 of 2?

Rule 2. The missions FOR the road are mutual God-human/ human-God relationships and universal human-God-human relationships.

Not only is the combined rule shorter - would the reader agree? - It avoids the conflictual confusion of ranking.

Tuesday February 19, 2008

Relationships

Before we move on leaving two short rules only FOR the infrastructure and mission of the Road to the Incomprehensible God of the Universe we should be certain that we are of one accord on the term: relationships.

Rule 1. The road to the Incomprehensible God of the Universe is open to ALL who breathe. The Incomprehensible God of the Universe is the atmosphere of possibilities.

Rule 2. The missions FOR the road are mutual God-human/ human-God relationships and universal human-God-human relationships.

The Relationship of Incomprehensible God to the Universe:

The term atmosphere of possibilities is not a delineation of the form of the Incomprehensible God. It is an ethereal description of the functions of that God in relationship to the Cosmos and to evolving life wherever it occurs within the Universe.

The relationship of Incomprehensible God to life:

Because the human is beginning to decipher aspects of the initiation and evolution of the Cosmos and the initiation and evolution of life, is no indication that the human can ever decipher the relationship between Incomprehensible God and comprehensible life. Over the millennia as humans have faced this indecipherable relationship many have solved the dilemma for themselves by dropping God from the equation. If there is no God - there is no problem. Beyond dropping God, some still want to expend energy on the matter so they try to sell the God-free equation to others. In recent centuries this has proven quite a boon to the publishing business.

Another false solution: For at least four millennia the Judeo/ Christian religion has solved the dilemma of the God-human/ human-God relationship by transforming the Incomprehensible God of the Universe to a Comprehensible God of the Bible verse. One problem is that within this transformation the equation's main constant, God is love, is either obscured within the verses or lost within centuries of interpreting the verses. A second problem is that the sacred writings become the very idol that the writings warn against.

Within the God-human half of this love relationship we have come to assign the code word grace to God's participation. Within the human-God half of the love relationship we have come to assign several code words to the human's participation: they range from reverence and trust to awe and fear. How about agape (selfless love)?

In the next blog we'll look at the human-God-human relationship.

Tuesday, February 26, 2008

Human-God-Human

It would be so simple to speak of two relationships: God/human and human/human. It would be simple, but totally inadequate. That is why it is necessary to expand the term God/human relationship to the more descriptive, mutual, two way relationship: God-human/human-God.

The term human/human relationship is descriptive of physical, sociological relationships within the species but ignores being response-able to the fulfilling atmosphere of possibilities. Thus it is vital to remind humans of the metaphysical nature of existence. This is most simply done by inserting the metaphysical term God into human/human relationships: human-God-human.

And here we arrive at a dilemma!

The human perspectives I bring to the dilemma differ from the perspectives you bring to the dilemma.

This is a problem. Fortunately, in varying degrees we, as an intelligent species, are gradually coming to avoid, or analyze and correct, some of these differences.

But there is an even greater problem. When the two sides claim to include God as we approach a dilemma we bring differing messages from our differing, humanly created Gods.

Just as humans hold differing perspectives, they claim differing Gods.

Is the Comprehensible God of the Bible verse different from the Incomprehensible God of the Universe? Of course not. The differences derive from our contraries on the functions and forms of the same God.

This is why in the 1950s J.B. Phillips (Bishop John Bertram Phillips) wrote the wonderful little book, "Your God Is Too Small." His apologetic was not that we have Gods of varying size or power. He was observing that we diminish the One God by portraying God's form and functions through factious doctrines and fictitious miracles painted by priests. kings and all of us.... with tiny, human brushes. (paraphrase of John Adams)

What a dilemma we have created within the human-God-human relationship. How do today's humans remorph the Judeo-Christian religion through which previous humans molded (then remolded) nature's Incomprehensible God into humanity's Comprehensible God?

We have arrived at this dilemma through stories, commandments, miracles, doctrines, tenets - ad infinitum.

How can I be so naive as to suggest that we can navigate the Road to the Incomprehensible God of the Universe by following two miniscule Rules OF the Road?

I'll try in the next blog.

Tuesday March 4, 2008

Rules OF the Road

The purpose for the Road to the Incomprehensible God of the Universe can be expressed as two Rules FOR the Road:

Rule 1. FOR the Road. The road to the Incomprehensible God of the Universe is for ALL who breathe. The Incomprehensible God of the Universe is the atmosphere of possibilities. (Holmes Rolston, III)

Rule 2. FOR the Road. The missions FOR the road are mutual God-human/human-God relationships and universal human-God-human relationships.

How do we transpose the Rules (Purpose) FOR the Road to Rules (Protocol) OF the Road? The protocol of the Road to the Comprehensible God of the Universe can be expressed as two Rules OF the Road.

Rule 1. OF the Road: All humans may travel the road.

Rule 2. OF the Road: All travelers can share two congruent missions: (a.) To be response-able to the Incomprehensible God of the Universe* and (b.) To act responsibly toward all of humanity.**

> * The response-able mission of humans to God is worship expressed as stewardship.

> ** The responsible mission of humans to humans is kinship (expressed as agape love).

P.S. I would prefer to use the word "evangelism" (spreading the Good News of the Incomprehensible God of the Universe) rather than "agape love," but Christians have long since linked the word evangelism possessively and specifically to the Comprehensible God of the Bible verse.

Tuesday, March 11, 2008

Three Realities

The November 1, 2007 Blog noted that immediately upon reaching the mountaintop in our journey of faith we are confronted by a road which forks. I stated it this way:

"Here I am. I have climbed Martin Luther King's mountain and can see the road to the To-Be-Known Land just ahead. Immediately

I see a fork in the road. Do I follow Yogi Berra's advice? "When you come to a fork in the road - take it."

No, it is not that simple. Especially when the two road signs read:

Road to the Comprehensible God of the Bible Verse.
Road to the Incomprehensible God of the Universe."

Several blogs have been offered to develop the metaphors of two differing faith journeys as two roads: one to a vision of Nature's God (the Incomprehensible God of the Universe), another to a vision of the Bible's God (the Comprehensible God of the Bible Verse). The author has been unsubtle, yes, even clumsy, as he has presented the case that if the church continues breathing air tainted by factious doctrines and fictitious miracles (Adams), rather than the atmosphere of possibilities (Ralston), its chances of survival will remain diminished.

I have not stated that the church will "die." I have not threatened that, unless humans choose one road over the other, they will "die," as in "the God of the Bible Verse is the only road to salvation."

I have stated (inadequately) my belief that I am more comfortable with one road than the other and I would hope readers seize the opportunity to explore that road which presents as an "atmosphere of possibilities."

I recognize three realities within this exploration:

1. These blogs have been tedious reading for those whose leap of faith binds them steadfastly to their traditional, comprehensible God.

2. We are in a time of church decline wherein it is imperative to test all atmospheres of possibility that can morph the church to survival.

3. The task will be extremely difficult. Pray that we can all remain aware of God's ever present Good News within the process.

Monday, March 17, 2008

Reality 1.

1. These blogs have been tedious reading for those whose leap of faith binds them steadfastly to their traditional, comprehensible God.

This is understandable. Many times as I have wrestled with moving from the established tradition, the Comprehensible God of the Bible Verse, to a nebulous belief, the Incomprehensible God of the Universe, I have wondered why anyone, especially me, would impose such duress upon their being.

Just down the road from the country store where I grew up was a small Methodist Church. I did not learn to sing there. I have never learned to sing anywhere. But there I learned the tune and words of "Old Time Religion," or "That Old Time Religion," or "Give Me That Old Time Religion," or whichever of the other versions Google lists. I have carried one particular verse of the song from those days to this:

"It has saved our fathers." -- "It" being "That Old Time Religion."

This verse had to be sung as if the monosyllabic word "our" was really two syllables strung out as "ow ---- ur." When I think back to my age six struggle with solving the two syllable singing of "ow ---- ur" it gives me hope that I can work my way through transitioning from God the Comprehensible to God the Incomprehensible.

But reality brings me back from Cosmic cyberspace to my computer keyboard and I wonder how my transitioning belief system can be accurate when so many great minds have spent so many lifetimes accepting (or trying to prove true?) what increasingly appear to me to be factious doctrines and fictitious miracles.

Worse than this internal struggle, how do I dare approach traditionalists with this silly (in their minds) babble about morphing the Church so that it can survive? After all: "Give me that old time religion. It has saved ow ---- ur fathers."

OOPS!

It isn't the first person singular, "how do I dare to approach traditionalists?" It is the first person plural, "how do WE dare to approach traditionalists?

But - wait a moment. Perhaps the Church is diminishing because there are so many in this WE group?

Nor are WE approaching third person TRADITIONALISTS. Shouldn't it be stated as -- ALL OF US daring to reproach centuries of TRADITION............

SO THAT THE CHURCH CAN MORPH AND SURVIVE? Note: These ALL CAP words are residual to their being emphasized in a blog.

Thursday, March 27, 2008

Reality 2.

Reality 2. We are in a time of church decline wherein it is imperative to test those atmospheres of possibility that can morph the church to survival.

Over the centuries the church has faced periodic contumely.

Per my computer's dictionary:

contumely - noun. plural suffix - lies.

insolent or insulting language: example - the church should not be exposed to gossip and contumely.

I would add as a second dictionary example: "Nor should church members be exposed to gossip and contumely" e.g. over the centuries - stoning, crucifixion, burning at the stake, drowning, inquisition, excommunication, being branded apostate, denied the sacraments and on, and on, and on, and on.... church members have been subjected to contumely. All of these horrific contumelies were/are rendered in the name of the Comprehensible God of the Bible Verse.

Currently I would present a question that demonstrates and encompasses the many concerns related to the ongoing schism within my church, PCUSA. (Other churches may look to their examples.)

Does a religious interpretation which burns me at the stake do me any more eternal harm than one which tells me that my spiritual being is not acceptable to a Comprehensible God of the Bible Verse unless my belief system accepts innumerable, factious doctrines of that religion. e.g. The Bible is the infallible word of God. Christ is the only way to salvation?

Would that religion accept a comprehension that the Jesus of history does not bestow salvation as a surrogate of the Comprehensible God of the Bible Verse but is an example of how to be that human life which is response-able to the Incomprehensible God of the Universe, the atmosphere of possibilities, and is responsible within and to all of humanity, the breath of reality?

Of course, in the name of Christ, the church has been and has done many wonderful and rewarding and factually-miraculous things (as opposed to believing fictionally-miraculous things). Those of us who question some of the church's doctrines, which we see as shortcomings, are most thankful for this history. But we believe now is a time within developing humanity when the church must morph by inhaling the atmosphere of possibilities - if it is to survive.

Tuesday, April 01, 2008

Reality 3. Postponed

Reality 3. The task will be extremely difficult. Pray that we can all remain aware of God's ever present Good News within the process.

Not only will the morphing be extremely difficult, it will be of extremely long duration. In an earlier blog I ventured the 10,000 years from the hymn "Amazing Grace" as a guess. When one explores how long it has taken religion to arrive at today's point, 10,000 future years may be more minimal than rational.

Serendipity brought an article to my e-mail yesterday which is so appropriate to a discussion of the morphing's duration that I shall print it here and postpone Reality 3. to the next blog.

This is a Question from John Ford in Australia with an Answer from Bishop John Shelby Spong in America.

Question and Answer
With John Shelby Spong

John Ford, from Australia, writes via the Internet:

I have been fortunate enough to be a recipient of your newsletter for just a few months. I dropped in to your thesis on the Third Fundamental, which sent little shivers through me as you revealed something of which I had not been fully cognizant. Your words resonate with truth when you illustrate the nexus between God and evolution, in a way that I believe Pierre Teilhard de Chardin always did. My questions are "Are we going somewhere? Is there purpose driving evolution?" In other words, it would seem that a theology of God and evolution demands human responsibility to see that plan through to fruition. This changes the status quo somewhat, from patiently waiting to purposeful action. How say you? May God bless you and your ability to make connections.

(Here follows Bishop Spong's answer:)

Dear John,

Pierre Teilhard de Chardin was and is one of my favorite writers. You will find his work listed in most of my bibliographies, especially his book The Phenomenon of Man. De Chardin was both a priest and a paleontologist and was one of the earliest theological voices trying to bring the Christian faith into dialogue with the meaning of evolution.

His work was not appreciated by the still fearful hierarchy of the Roman Catholic Church, who placed his writings on the Index List, forbidding his work from being read by "the faithful." Thus it seems it will always be for those who step outside of theological boxes to engage "new ideas."

De Chardin does believe that there is an evolving spirit, that human beings have a way yet to travel before they are able to embrace the fullness of the "Transcendent Consciousness." He sees Jesus as having achieved a kind of spiritual or consciousness breakthrough. De Chardin has always been more popular with people on a spiritual quest than with those who somehow believe that they are in possession of the full and ultimate truth of God.

For me, I am convinced that the pilgrimage of our lives is into deeper consciousness and deeper humanity. I have the feeling that 100 or 500 or 1,000 years from now our generation will be regarded as somewhat primitive.

John Shelby Spong

Wednesday, April 9, 2008

Reality 3.

Reality 3. The task will be extremely difficult. Pray that we can all remain aware of God's ever present Good News within the process.

We are back from the blogging detour that took us to Bishop Spong's Q&A which in turn gave us the following noteworthy quote:

"For me, I am convinced that the pilgrimage of our lives is into deeper consciousness and deeper humanity. I have the feeling that 100 or 500 or 1,000 years from now our generation will be regarded as somewhat primitive."

John Shelby Spong

At least Bishop Spong's estimate is more optimistic than the 10,000 years I ventured in my previous blog.

When I found the name of Teilhard deChardin in the Spong blog, I was reminded of the rewarding hours I spent forty years ago working my way through deChardin's "Phenomenon of Man." I went to my shelf and there it was, right where it belonged, very close to J.B. Phillips', "Your God Is Too Small."

In the 1970's when I completed my study of "The Phenomenon of Man" and placed it on the shelf, I found myself acknowledging de Chardin as "a proponent of the vision of humanity at the tiller of the world." (A current quote from Wikipedia)

Here follows deChardin's statement that I have retained from that previous reading: "Man has grabbed the tiller of the world."

I was not ready then, nor am I ready now, to grant humanity full control of the tiller. However I am much more aware now than I was then that God is not a gray bearded pilot holding the tiller with the same hand that Michelangelo depicted creating Adam in the painting on the ceiling of the Sistine Chapel.

In these days of Global Warming, even if we cannot comprehend how the tiller is shared, we are surely aware that the human hand needs metaphysical skills for the task. Likewise we humans must search beyond the Comprehensible God of the Bible Verse to discover the atmosphere of possibilities available from the Incomprehensible God of the Universe.

Now, as I reread deChardin's "The Phenomenon of Man," I find him making this prophetic statement in the Twentieth Century:

"Our century is probably more religious than any other. How could it fail to be, with such problems to be solved? The only trouble is that it has not yet found a God it can adore."

Teilhard deChardin, The Phenomenon of Man.

I think I understand what de Chardin means by "a God it [humanity] can adore." However humans often describe the same thought in differing words.

As proof of differing words I want to close this specific blog with some differing but very sage words which came to me as comment on one of my previous blogs.

Dear Ed -

I am reading a book called Christianity for the Rest of Us. (Diana Butler Bass) The author wrote it based on a study of some 50 churches of various denominations and in various geographical locations; 10 of them were studied more deeply. I was interested in the section on Purple Churches in which the people are both Republican and Democrat, vote in diverse ways in the political arena but come to church and pray together and work together toward justice and peace in the community. They have found something, a spirit, a life of prayer, a belief in God, something that transcends their temporal differences and is distinctly "Christian".

One can see similar changes in how Christianity is understood as related to science. Not all biblical Christians are fundamentalists, eschewing science.

I don't think transcendence has to mean supernatural anymore. It seems to me the church is evolving, even as you are seeking the morphing, a more dramatic change. Those are my thoughts.

Oh, and good morning!!

Sara

Monday, April 14, 2008

More on Reality 3.

Reality 3. The task will be extremely difficult. Pray that we can all remain aware of God's ever present Good News within the process.

What is the task? Is the task to save the Christian Church that must change (evolve? morph?) or die? Well, yes, partially . . . but the true task is for all humanity to transfer humanity's religious belief systems from various Comprehensible Gods of multiple books and verses to the Incomprehensible God of the Universe.

What is the Good News? The Good News is that the Incomprehensible God of the Universe relates temporally to all of humanity in this real life and ethereally in an extended "life" beyond human comprehension.

I recently read a thoughtful editorial ("Elder elders, engage!") in the magazine "Presbyterian Outlook,"
(March 24, 2008). Editor Jack Haberer was encouraging aging Presbyterian elders in three specific ways: 1. Do not assume that oncoming generations within the church will have better answers. 2.

Do not become "stuck" in the mind sets of any previous era. 3. Think outside of, beyond, the box.

This indicates to me the justified assumption that previous generations plus our current generations within the church have permitted, or encouraged, whatever it is within the box that is detracting religion from its part in the Good News.

There will be as many lists of the contents of the box as there are compilers. No two compilers will agree, hence I am bold enough to offer my list:

Category A. Factious Fundamentals and Doctrines.
Category B. Embellished Stories and Myths.
Category C. Outmoded Knowledge and Cultures.

The A, B, C listing intends no chronological or qualitative priorities.

There is no purity to these categories. There are of course many cross references.

I have not stated that the church will "die." I have not threatened that humans who choose one road over the other will be denied eternal life, as in this statement:

"The Christ of the Bible Verse is the only way to salvation."

I have stated (inadequately) my belief that I am more comfortable with one road than the other and I would hope readers seize the opportunity to explore that same road as one which presents to them as an "atmosphere of possibilities."

I repeat the three realities, given earlier, pertinent to this exploration:

> 1. These blogs have been tedious reading for those whose leap of faith binds them steadfastly to their traditional, comprehensible God.

2. We are in a time of church decline wherein it is imperative to test all atmospheres of possibility that can morph the church to survival.

3. The task will be extremely difficult. Pray that we can all remain aware of God's ever present Good News within the process.

One time I heard a challenging lecture in a continuing education course on being creative. Here is a quote from the course presenter, Jay Yanoff:

"To be truly creative, one must break mental sets and think beyond reality."

I would suggest that to discover our response-ableness to the Incomprehensible God of the Universe we must break our mental sets with the Comprehensible God of the Bible verse (see Categories A, B and C above) and think beyond pseudo-reality. I would venture further that this pseudo-reality fills the box that we are so often admonished to think beyond.

Next will be a brief blog on why morphing continues to fail.

Monday, April 21, 2008

Why Morphing Is Difficult.

A serious comment from a sage peer, expressed in the form of four questions, has recently come to me.

a. Exactly what is it that you advocate morphing?
b. Is it the Presbyterian Church in the USA?
c. Is it the Christian Church in the World?

d. Is it the All in All of human religion?"

I've given this comment (these questions) much thought. Here are my answers plus time line projections.

a. Currently it is my personal belief system. (Timeline = my lifetime)
b. Eventually yes, the Presbyterian Church in the USA. (Timeline unknown)
c. Eventually yes, the Christian Church in the World. (Timeline unknown)
d. Eventually yes, the All in All of Human Religion. (Timeline Infinity)

How do we morph our personal belief systems? Each individual invests her/his mental, physical, spiritual self into, and trusts his/her mental, physical, spiritual self to, the Atmosphere of Possibilities. That is to say - becomes response-able to the Incomprehensible God of the Universe.

Why is it difficult to morph our individual belief systems?

I suggest that we within the church fail because we have continued to breathe a depleted atmosphere lacking possibilities. We have refused to abandon rigid mental sets related to the Comprehensible God of the Bible Verse and thus fail to discover flexible possibilities available from the Incomprehensible God of the Universe.

This calls for exploring out into the Atmosphere of Possibilities -- beyond the ABC contents of the box (See April 14, 2008 blog).

Why is it difficult for groups to morph communal belief systems?

Murphy's Law of Change (per this author) : It is much easier for an individual to effect change than for groups to decide what change to effect.

Perhaps we have stumbled into a partial answer to our question?

Monday. April 28, 2008

Enemies and Ghosts.

In December, 2007 I toyed with the idea of attempting to establish, through statistical evidence, that the church is moving toward morphing.

This might sound like a good idea except for the reality that greater statistical evidence seems to indicate that the church is moving toward schism and a lingering, debilitating death.

In recent blogs I have reasoned that if we could determine the contents of the "box," the impeding contents we are constantly admonished to think beyond, we could empty the box of its impediments, recharge it with "the right stuff," and morph us onto the Road to the Incomprehensible God of the Universe.

I was prepared to spend a blog or two on exploring why we have so much difficulty changing, reforming, evolving, morphing . . . personal and communal belief systems -- establishing an answer -- and moving on.

Now, in this early morning hour, as I sat down to blog this blog, I found these words of Walt Kelly's character Pogo appearing on the monitor -

"We have met the enemy and he is us."
And following this statement came these words:
"We have opened the box and it is full of. . . ghosts."

The reader may remember that in my "self-proclaimed, infinite wisdom" in the April 14, 2008 blog I presented my ABC listing of the contents of the "box."

"There will be as many lists of the contents of the box as there are compilers. No two compilers will agree, hence I am bold enough to offer my list:
Category A. Factious Fundamentals and Doctrines.

Category B. Embellished Stories and Myths.
Category C. Outmoded Knowledge and Cultures."

I was wrong. I was thinking in the real/surreal mode -- reality vs. surreality. The "box" (the "impediment box") is actually full of ghosts:

Ghosts of physical existence - the true vs. the false.

Ghosts of psychological existence - the acceptable vs. the unacceptable.

Ghosts of metaphysical existence - all totally inexorable and undefinable.

All three types of ghosts can be, or are, box contents which serve as impediments within the, "to be thought beyond," box.

The human is capable of accepting the real and thinking beyond the surreal ghosts of the physical and psychological.

e.g. physical - Some physical facts are true, some are false. The sun does not revolve around the earth.

e.g. psychological - Both genes and environments contribute to behaviors, some of which are more acceptable than others.

The human is not capable of determining between the real and the surreal ghosts of the metaphysical.

e.g. metaphysical - NO human mind can comprehend, define, or know better than other human minds, the metaphysical.

Metaphysical "reality" hatches in one mind and then tradition deposits its eggs in incubating minds - and every human mind is an incubator. ALL metaphysical ghosts are imaginary.

If God is love and the human is created in that image why would God appear as an unloving ghost in some minds? . . . a ghost prompting those minds to believe that there is only one way to salvation (eternal metaphysical life) and denied to all others.

If God is love such prompting is imaginary or it is coming from a ghost which that mind is imagining.

Splinters, splits, schisms -- ineptitudes, intolerance, inquisitions - are the work of imaginary metaphysical ghosts. These are the ghosts we must think beyond. These are the ghosts that inhibit our breathing the "Atmosphere of Possibilities."

Where am I in my attempt to morph my belief system? I am closing in on a "Belief System for the Uninhibited."

Tuesday, May 06, 2008

KNOWing God

Publishing a blog on the internet differs from presenting an essay or an apologetic in print. My blogging program will not permit the use of italics for emphasis. It will permit the use of quotation marks but they are not a satisfactory substitute.

Once a supportive editor advised me that putting too many words (or phrases) in quotation marks [or brackets] in print is as "destructive" as inserting the words "you know" too many times in speech. Observe the previous sentence. See what the editor meant?

Also, in the e-mail and blogging world, it has come to be acceptable to use words with all CAPS for emphasis. SEE what I mean?

Some blogs come to very difficult stages in construction. Last week's blog arrived at such a point. How does a blogger make the point that the human is simply not capable of comprehending the nature of God?

The following excerpt from last week's blog framed in quotes is an example of an attempt.

"The human is not capable of determining between the real and the surreal ghosts of the metaphysical.

e.g. metaphysical - NO human mind can comprehend, define, or know better than other human minds, the metaphysical."

I wrote last weeks blog and spent some days trying to adjust it to convey my point that the human mind is simply not capable of comprehending the nature of God. I finally published the blog, following through on the theme that thinking beyond the box means thinking beyond ghosts of what may or may not be real within the physical and the psychological. But when it comes to defining the metaphysical all human descriptions of God are imaginations, ghosts of the surreal.

Please note in the e.g. metaphysical quote, a few lines above, the NO in caps. For several days of review I had the word KNOW in that same space in caps. In some humans' minds they do believe that they KNOW God better than other humans do. Perhaps this is because they have established, and follow, a set of standards that render them more response-able to God than other humans are -- in their own comprehension.

Do we KNOW God in our minds or do we KNOW God in our pinches of image spirit? The common expression is, "In our hearts." Did God give some humans bigger, better pinches than others? Would that God be love?

I suffer varying reactions to that tempting force which whispers in my ear that I KNOW God better than those others who hold different standards.

I continue toward a belief system for the uninhibited.

Monday, May 12, 2008

Searching for the Uninhibited

A couple of years ago I wrote a small book titled "A Belief System from the General Store."

No, I did not purchase a belief system at the general store where most of the necessities for rural living were sold. I learned a belief system from my always honest and most times saintly grandmother and family who owned and ran the store and from the men of the community who loafed there. These men were mostly honest and saintly. Like all of us a few were sometimes less than that in both departments.

As Yogi Berra says, "You can observe a lot by watching." Between the sidewalk seminars with the loafers and group discussions with my father, mother, grandmother and two sisters I learned most everything I needed to know, although I never went to kindergarten. I would say, however, that much of the foundation for my belief system was established before I started first grade at age 5.

Before I mislead the reader to assume that this was an ideal belief system incubator, I must tell you about one of our customers.

There were no rural power lines in our area but our house and store were served by a 32 volt Delco power plant in a small structure built onto the store. This generator connected with two long lines of green-glass, acid- filled batteries in the cellar of the store. When a large drain on the electrical system, like a refrigerator, kicked in the lights would dim.

One night a recent newcomer to the community was in the store when the lights dimmed. His reaction, "The lights dim just like that in the penitentiary back where I come from when they electrocute somebody."

My grandmother and I looked at each other but our good manners held us back from asking him how he had come by this information.

Another time he told me that if you scratched a sore with your forefinger it would not heal, so you should always use the next finger. I fear I honored that therapeutic gem until health class in high school.

So you see, not all that I learned in the general store was good for the belief system. Many of the ghosts in our boxes of inhibitions, that we are ofttimes admonished to think beyond, were placed there by hyper-imaginative folks who were trying to help us.

In fact over the centuries all cultural and religious groups have been exposed to many questionable inhibitions aimed at a better quality of life for their members. Seems to me that too many inhibitions aimed at making us better have the potential for converting into aberrations making us believe that indeed we are better -- better than others, especially those whose belief systems differ from ours.

I feel that I am closer year by year, week by week, day by day to a belief system for the uninhibited.

Sunday, May 18, 2008

Blessed Are the Uninhibited

The reader will remember that recently I reported messages appearing on my computer monitor at an early morning hour.

The first message: "We have met the enemy and he is us."

The second message: "We have opened the box and it is full. . . of ghosts."

It is again early in the morning. Today there is another message. This one is from an unknown source - not the plural, personal pronoun, "We," source indicating physical and psychological human involvement. This message starts out with a blessing as if it comes from beyond humanity - from the metaphysical? However, no divine revelation is indicated, or claimed.

This third message connects the present to the future:

"Blessed are the Uninhibited for they shall recognize the Atmosphere of Possibilities."

Who are the Uninhibited?

Another time recently I reported that I was closing in on a Belief System for the Uninhibited. The Uninhibited are those persons not inhibited by the contents of the box that we are to think beyond, the box with its ABC contents and its Ghosts. See blog, "Enemies and Ghosts," April 28, 2008.

What is the Atmosphere of Possibilities?

This is the metaphor that Holmes Rolston III uses in his book, "Genes, Genesis and God, Their Origins in Natural and Human History," to describe the Nature of the Incomprehensible God of the Universe as the Atmosphere of Possibilities.

This is not to say that those inhibited by comprehensible metaphors of the Nature of the God of the Bible Verse cannot recognize the Atmosphere of Possibilities.

However, it is to say, that too often, the claim of comprehending the ABCs:

A. Factious Fundamentals and Doctrines.
B. Embellished Stories and Myths.
C. Outmoded Knowledge and Cultures.

abrogates, blocks, the claimant's opportunities to recognize the Atmosphere of Possibilities.

"Blessed are the Uninhibited for they shall recognize the Atmosphere of Possibilities."

Friday, May 30, 2008

It's Beyond the Box

As I go back to the first blog that I released into cyberspace, I discover that the date was May 27, 2005 and the title was, "It's Beyond Me."

As I scan forward through the Archives of all the postings to the present, I find that two major themes have developed synergistically:

1. That segment of the formal religious establishment described loosely by the term church, is under stress. The extreme nature of this stress is demonstrated by the current, often-quoted, fearsome phrase - "The Church must change or it will die."

2. The most frequently offered response to this dilemma is the admonition, "We must think beyond the box."

Pragmatism indicates that: "The Church must change or it will die" phrase is hopelessly destructive. Might this prediction be more approachable if rephrased as? "The Church must morph, then survive."

Survival indicates that: It is essential that we determine what it is in the box that we must think beyond.

In the April 9, 2008 blog and repeated in the May 18, 2008 blog I suggested that the major elements within the box fall into three categories. Here repeated, the three are listed as the ABCs of the box:

    A. Factious Fundamentals and Doctrines.
    B. Embellished Manifestations and Myths.
    C. Outmoded Knowledge and Cultures.

The categories sampled and demonstrated:

A. Factious Fundamentals and Doctrines.

Factions within the Church hold to fundamentals and doctrines at variance with those held by other factions within the Church.

e.g. A factious fundamental - God chose/elects certain peoples over others.

e.g. A factious doctrine - Jesus Christ is the only way to salvation. Factious holdings of this nature generate conflict.

The church must morph beyond these conflicts to survive.

B. Embellished Manifestations and Myths.

Many manifestations and myths offered as proof of specific beliefs about God contradict the supreme manifestation that God is Love. Why would innocent, first born Egyptians, still children, have to die as part of a successful, God led Exodus?

Why would God devise (or permit) the death of the Ultimately Response-Able Jesus as the atonement for human sin?

C. Outmoded Knowledge and Cultures.

Energy and effort are required to be adequately enlightened in this age of rapidly expanding knowledge.

However - this expended energy is miniscule compared to the deficit in quality of life that we impose on our progeny when we transmit outmoded knowledge and cultures.

Now. . . Do we morph the contents of the box we are to think beyond, or should we morph our systems through which we believe?

Here I shall enter a most personal note. Over the past few years I have seen my belief system morph from a God I believed I could comprehend, perhaps even "understand the nature of," the Comprehensible God of the Bible Verse, to a God I cannot comprehend or understand the nature of, the Incomprehensible God of the Universe.

This has been wrenching but not painful. Wrenching because of my innate fear that others could not/would not accept one undergoing such a morphing. Not painful because I had finally come to the awareness that my faith had to risk a leap beyond the box containing the Comprehensible God of the Bible verse.

What does morphing ones belief system entail?

We morph our belief systems from the Comprehensible God of the Bible Verse to the Incomprehensible God of the Universe by breathing the Atmosphere of Possibilities* - within which the human can be response-able to God and responsible toward all of humanity, including self.

Therefore, a suggested belief statement from beyond the box:

I believe that the Incomprehensible God of the Universe is an Atmosphere of Possibilities within which the human can be a response-able steward to/for God and responsible to all of humanity, including self.

One conclusion in four parts:

The box beyond which we "must think" will always contain factious fundamentals and doctrines because there will always be unique human factions.

The unique human intellect is capable of embellishing any manifestations and myths.

The unique human intellect is capable of retaining any outmoded knowledge and cultures.

The church will morph and survive because God is an available atmosphere of possibilities beyond any box that we humans construct.

* "The divine spirit is the giver of life, pervasively present over the millennia. God is the atmosphere of possibilities, the metaphysical environment, in, with, and under first the natural and later also the cultural environment, luring the Earthen histories upslope." (p.367)
Genes, Genesis, and God. Their Origins in Natural and Human History.
by Holmes Rolston III

Thursday, June 05, 2008

Two Adjustments

Statement # 1. "The Church will morph when enough of its adherents develop belief systems that recognize the Atmosphere of Possibilities." (Final sentence from the blog titled "Blessed are the Uninhibited," published May 18, 2008.)

Statement # 2. "The church will morph and survive because God is an available atmosphere of possibilities beyond any box that we humans construct." (Final sentence from the blog titled "Beyond the Box," published May 30, 2008.)

As I review these two statements neither is totally accurate within the context of the ultimate intent of my words.

Statement # 1. should read: "The Church will (begin to) morph when enough of its adherents develop belief systems that recognize the Atmosphere of Possibilities."

Statement # 2. should read: "The church will (be able to) morph and survive because God is an available atmosphere of possibilities beyond any box that we humans construct."

"The difference between the almost right word & the right word is really a large matter--it's the difference between the lightning bug and the lightning." Mark Twain.

In the first statement the difference is that of time. In the second statement the difference that of condition.

As corrected both statements bring me to the position wherein I feel comfortable with the state of the belief systems of those who would morph the church.

Per statement #1: I am persuaded that many of the uninhibited are ready (ANXIOUS) to live their unique "I" version of the following belief statement:

"I believe that the Incomprehensible God of the Universe is an Atmosphere of Possibilities within which the human can be a response-able steward to/for God and responsible to all of humanity, including self."

Per statement #2: I am persuaded further that with sufficient members thinking beyond the box the church can (WILL) morph beyond the box and survive.

Next week I shall start to explore what I hope we can be persuaded to DO.

Monday, June 9, 2008

Persuaded to DO?

As I pondered answers to, "What can we be persuaded to DO?" it occurred to me that it would be interesting to search the web for responses to the phrase, "I am persuaded."

I did. (Google) Results - about 725,000 for "I am persuaded." (Yahoo) Results - about 21,400,000 for "I am persuaded."

I am persuaded to be amazed.

Is this why we must think beyond the box? There is no room left for thought in the box. It is crammed with persuasions from persuaders trying to persuade.

Thousands upon thousands of: fundamentals, doctrines, manifestations, laws, tenets, scruples, catechisms, creeds, dogmas, precepts, principles, articles, canons, maxims, rules, convictions, ad infinitum -- plus 22,125,000 "I am persuadeds."

This exercise convinces me persuasion is a very crowded field at the moment and it is most difficult to persuade others to DO. Therefore I shall make no attempt to persuade. I shall share. I shall share what I have come to accept as my belief system from beyond the box.

My "beyond the box" claim makes no claim beyond this one - "It works for me."

The belief statement that I offer here to explain this system is only a template, a model to be tailored to suit each unique individual. It is this:

"I believe that the Incomprehensible God of the Universe is an Atmosphere of Possibilities within which the human can be a response-able steward to/for the Incomprehensible God and responsible to all of humanity, including self."

What if those persons who would help morph the church developed their unique, personal versions of this suggested, belief system?

What if those persons who would help morph the church ignored most of these thousands upon thousands of . . . fundamentals, doctrines, manifestations, laws, tenets, scruples, catechisms, creeds, dogmas, precepts, principles, articles, canons, maxims, rules, convictions, ad infinitum?

What if those persons who would help morph the church accepted the five following precepts derived from this Incomprehensible God Belief System?

1. The Incomprehensible God of the Universe is a leap of faith beyond the box containing the Comprehensible God of the Bible Verse.

2. The God capable of morphing the church to survival is An Atmosphere of Possibilities beyond the boxes wherein humankind stores its anthropomorphic God(s).

3. To be response-able to the God of the Universe the human must be a steward of the Universe. Stewardship is the ultimate expression of worship.

4. Within the Atmosphere of Possibilities the only way to be response-able to God is to be responsible to all of humanity.

5. Within the Atmosphere of Possibilities the only way to be responsible to all of humanity is to be responsible to a response-able self.

Can one very brief belief statement and five short, supporting precepts prepare us to begin morphing the church?

Monday, June 16, 2008

Yes, they can.

Can one very brief belief statement and five short, supporting precepts prepare us to begin morphing the church?
Yes, they can ... with two small caveats.

A. Those who would morph the church to survival shall recognize their version of Incomprehensible God of the Universe as the Atmosphere of Possibilities within which they are now free to believe and act.

B. Those who would morph the church to survival shall recognize that cultures and traditions have too long confined the Comprehensible God of the Bible Verse to anthropomorphic boxes beyond which they are now free to believe and act.

I am persuaded,
that we are prepared,
to begin discussing:
morphing the church.

Sunday, June 22, 2008

Morphing the Church

Why is it we are persuaded to morph the church? "The church must morph to survive." This is a statement, but it is not an answer. It avoids the epicenter question, "Why is the church dying?"

We have talked about the box and its ABCs we must think beyond, we have contrasted the Comprehensible God of the Bible Verse with the Incomprehensible God of the Universe, we have overused the word anthropomorphic as in -- constraining comprehension of God to the box, we have touched on suffocation via contumelies and resuscitation via the Atmosphere of Possibilities -- but what exactly is it that is causing the church to die?

How is the life of the human maintained? Blood is the transport system that delivers life-giving oxygen within the human body. This blood must be "just right" in consistency, in cellular and chemical content.

How is the life of the church maintained? Religion connects the church body to the Atmosphere of Possibilities. Like functioning blood, the oxygen transporter in the human body; religion, the belief transporter in the church body, must be "just right" as in "optimal use" for the church to live. "Over use" or "under use" or "misuse" can all result in abuse.

Here I pause for a definition:

religion, n. a system of faith or belief - example; "the great religions of the world."

I would venture that this definition is inadequate. A system is a self-contained unit. Religion is more than a system. Religion is the supernatural conductor connecting individual and communal belief systems to God, the Atmosphere of Possibilities, the Metaphysical Oxygen.

Church bodies die when they "stray" too far from the optimal, response-able relationship of their communal belief systems with the Atmosphere of Possibilities.

What does "stray" mean?" To stray is to wander away from our base beliefs - our personal belief systems or our communal body of belief, whether we use church or some other term to designate a body of believers.

Each unique human has a pinch of response-able spirit that connects with the Incomprehensible God of the Universe, the Atmosphere of Possibilities. I can describe that connection for myself but I cannot define or design it for others.

"Say nothing of my religion," said Thomas Jefferson. "It's known to my God and myself alone."

However, I can present as a template, not as a dictate, the basis of my belief system:

"I believe that the Incomprehensible God of the Universe is an Atmosphere of Possibilities within which the human can be a response-able steward to/for the Incomprehensible God and responsible to all of humanity, including self."

I feel comfortable using this belief statement as an example of the zenith point from which we can measure straying.

Churches and larger belief groups stay on course when their religious practices are optimal and attuned to the Atmosphere of Possibilities. Such groups stray when overuse or underuse or misuse of these practices lead to abuse of their being response-able to God or being responsible to humanity.

In the next blog we will look at some examples of these abuses.

Thursday, July 3. 2008

The Abuse of Religion:101a.

It is easy to abuse religion.

Religion can be abused with too much trying. (overuse)
Religion can be abused with too little trying. (underuse)
Religion can be abused without even trying,   (misuse)

It is impossible to name, list or even categorize the plethora of specifics or generalities that abuse religion. But, on the other hand, it is impossible to determine what is causing the death of the church without having a grasp of what is abusing religion. This is referred to as a Catch 22.

I am going to pick three areas where confrontation has overwhelmed discussion and is creating the abuse of religion.

I shall present these areas by quoting from a web site: http://confessingchurch.homestead.com/contacts.html

A quote from the Home Page of that web site:

"The Confessing Church Movement
Within The Presbyterian Church (USA)

Proclaiming The Historic Christian Confessions Of The Reformed Faith

The Confessing Church Movement
Within The Presbyterian Church (USA)

This Web Site Is A Service Of The Presbyterian Layman

Welcome to the Web site about the Confessing Church Movement within the Presbyterian Church (USA).

This site provides news, information, resources and other material -- including contact information about congregations -- as a service to those who are taking a stand by proclaiming their commitment to three essential doctrines:

> 1. That Jesus Christ alone is Lord of all and the way of salvation.

2. That holy Scripture is the Triune God's revealed Word, the Church's only infallible rule of faith and life.

3. That God's people are called to holiness in all aspects of life. This includes honoring the sanctity of marriage between a man and a woman, the only relationship within which sexual activity is appropriate."

The following statement in quotes is from the material above: "... those who are taking a stand by proclaiming their commitment to three essential doctrines:"

Could this position and the three statements listed, contribute to the box (remember the box?) which some still cannot permit thinking beyond? Could naming these three statements "essential doctrines" place them in the box as: Category A. Factious Fundamentals and Doctrines?

It is sheer coincidence that each of these three statements defined by their believers as essential doctrines appears to match a separate one of the three ways to abuse religion (overuse, underuse, misuse).

This blog will deal with the first part of this threesome:

Religion can be abused with too much trying. (overuse)

There are so many specifics and generalities here -- where do we start? I shall start with what many humans see as the delicate balance between being response-able to God and being responsible to humanity. Over all of human history, since an awareness of the religious nature of the dual connectedness with God and with fellow humans, the human has tried to justify helping (too often - forcing) his/her fellows to relate to God in the same fashion she/he relates to God.

From whence cometh this justification?

"God's revealed truth."

More commonly it is stated this way: "Long, long ago, God inspired someone that this should be done and now, for me to be religious, I must do it."

In the meantime God inspired someone else to record that, "God is love." Could it be possible that God would love someone who doesn't relate to God in the fashion I do? Where is my responsibility to that person?

If God chooses some, does God reject others? We've had unknown numbers of angels dance to that tune on the head of a pin before.

If my religious body, e.g. my church, states that, "Jesus Christ alone is Lord of all and the way of salvation," is that an overuse of religion? placing all others outside the God is love formula?

If over 62% of the members of my national church believe there is no hell but the denomination still states in worship as creedal that Christ descended into hell - is that an outmoded overuse of religion?

If portions of the Bible contradict that God is love but my church demands that I idolize the Bible as infallible is that an overuse of religion?

Does the reader join me in finding it strange that, in this time of enlightenment, it is vital to help the church morph away from the overuse of outmoded religious concepts?

Wednesday, July 9, 2008

The Abuse of Religion 101b.

It is easy to abuse religion. Religion can be abused with too little trying. (underuse)

In my belief statement template I propose that the human acts as a steward of the universe when being response-able to God. In another place (Precept # 3 of 5 beyond the belief template) I describe stewardship as the ultimate act of worship. Thus in contradistinction, one can say that inadequate or inappropriate stewardship demonstrate the underuse of religion.

How does this relate to Confessing Church statement #2, labeled an essential doctrine by that movement?

> 2. That holy Scripture is the Triune God's revealed Word, the Church's only infallible rule of faith and life.

In an era of enlightenment if one bases religion on outmoded knowledge and cultures from the past as opposed to visioning it within the atmosphere of possibilities in the present and future, one is at severe risk of underusing religion.

If one tries too much or tries too little to practice religion one can abuse it. Of the three manners in which the human can abuse religion, underuse probably brings the most abuse to the universe.

Overuses of religion which alter our responsibilities to humanity can be reversed, although painfully and over long periods of time. Abuses of religion that alter the universe can bring irreversible changes e.g. resource depletion, climate change, chemical and radiation contamination, nuclear winter, etc.

Helping morph the church to survival, when considered as part of morphing religion to survival on an endangered planet, with billions of humans, certainly should detract us from our fascination with books, creeds and doctrines that obsess on our being saved while billions perish.

Tuesday, July 15, 2008

The Abuse of Religion 101c.

It is so easy to abuse religion. We all can do it.
Religion can be abused without even trying, (misuse)

In no instance do we see religion suffering more turmoil or being subjected to more abuse than when we observe how the worldwide church is misusing religion as it tries to cope with all aspects of human sexuality.

The Number 3 statement listed by the Confessing Church Movement:

> "3. That God's people are called to holiness in all aspects of life. This includes honoring the sanctity of marriage between a man and a woman, the only relationship within which sexual activity is appropriate."

Sex has not been a heavy-duty subject in this series of blogs, but here we are and here sex is. When sex appears can sin be far behind?

Neither has the term "sin" been a large part of the content of this series of blogs. It is remarkable that the human capable of loving God and humanity is capable of ignoring God and harming humanity. Ignoring and harming are examples of sin.

If I touched on original sin it was only to deny its validity as a concept. I digress but here is my position. If the concepts that God is love and God is the atmosphere of possibilities are true then the concept of original sin is moot.

One time an old sage shared his knowledge with me about snakes and sin. "There's big snakes and little snakes -- but sin is sin." (Of course this is silly, but --) Snakes are snakes and sin is sin but when it comes to sex and sin, they are too often uttered in the same sentence.

When the terms sanctity and marriage are used the use is not exclusively about sanctity or marriage. It is about all the other vagaries of human sexual behavior. I do not find it odd that the church has always been conflicted about human sexuality. Since before monotheism any myth that did not contain explicit sexual material did not make it to prime time. Oxygen transport is essential to life and hormones are vital to procreation.

So the church finds itself in knots over human sexuality. I do not want to dwell here nor do I want to appear simplistic or just plain simple. But -- it seems logical to me that when a man and a woman love each other and choose to consummate the union, they use the long established word marriage to define the consummation. So long as there is no physical or emotional harm to either party their sexual activity is their business.

It also seems logical to me that when a man loves a man or a woman loves a woman and they elect to consummate the union, they use some new word (merely for starters I would suggest - "joinage") to define the consummation. So long as there is no physical or emotional harm to either party - their sexual activity is their business.

In any instance the human, civil and religious rights are the same for all unions and the government and the church should respect them and get about their normal duties.

As for the many complexities that derive from the various human sexual behaviors, could we please stop searching the Bible for support of mass denigration and retribution and search the Atmosphere of Possibilities for case-by-case acceptance and compassion?

Sunday, July 20, 2008

A Catch-22?

This is not the concluding blog of my blogging, rather it is the summarizing blog of this series of blogs.

I approach summation as a catch-22. Here follows a brief Wickipedia definition:

"**Catch-22** is a term coined by Joseph Heller in his novel *Catch-22*, describing a false dilemma, where no real choice exists. In probability theory, it refers to a situation in which multiple probabilistic events exist, and the desirable outcome results from the confluence of these events, but there is zero probability of this happening, as they are mutually exclusive."

In this blog series I have presented material ultimately directed to two basic theses that can be abbreviated to the following statements:

1. The church must morph to survive.
2. To morph the church, we must think outside the box.

A minor Catch-22 is this:

Many of those who blog do not embrace these two topics as prime motivators, while many of those who hold these theses as vital do not blog.

Although there is no probability of the confluence of these two groups there is an outside solution: change the delivery medium from blog to book. A hard copy book is far better suited than blogs to reach those who are potential morphers.

We can morph these blogs into a book. I've given that consideration and I think I will do so.

Even with a book as a solution of the minor glitch we are still left with this major Catch-22:

Those who could/would morph the church do not think outside the box because the content of the box is what empowers them to be the church.

What is in the box? I've outlined this in previous blogs. I'll try again.

To comprehend God the human has developed theology to be the study of the nature of God. No one can verifiably claim to know the nature of God but the more who try, the greater the benefit to humankind, usually.

Anyone who thinks on the nature of God is a theologian. Professional or academic theologians simply spend more time at it than laypersons. The more comprehensible we make the nature of God the more readily we accept God and in turn the more easily we conjecture that God accepts us. Christians, to retain the long term comprehension of the nature of God within first the Jewish and later the Christian traditions, have compressed these comprehensions into the Bible. Although Christians may try to put God in the box - what they actually put in are their traditions and comprehensions.

However, when the human thinks of God as the Incomprehensible God of the Universe there is no way to compress that incomprehensibility into a box. That is why Holmes Rolston III has given us the proper term for the nature of God - The "Atmosphere of Possibilities, luring humankind upslope," and, dare I add? . . . "to think beyond the box."

Of course there are not two Gods - the Comprehensible and the Incomprehensible. But currently within Christianity there are two dominant perceptions of the nature of God, the Comprehensible God of the Bible Verse and the Incomprehensible God of the Universe.

God through humankind accomplishes many marvelous things, yes, even miraculous things, because there are response-able believers within each perception.

But . . . and here I end with a summary: "What if?"

"What if," all the energy humans waste on defending adverse perceptions could be combined into exploring diverse possibilities?

TFB 1. A Conundrum.

TFB = Theology for Beginners.

The time has come to start a new blog series – available on the web at this same address:

http://www.dejean.com/fromthegeneralstore/

The previous series of blogs came to conclusions that can be summarized in the following fashion:

- The Church must morph to survive.
- To morph the Church its members must morph their belief systems.
- To morph their belief systems members must think beyond the box containing factious myths and doctrines about the Comprehensible God of the Bible Verse, the Climate of Cultures, to search out how to become response-able to the Incomprehensible God of the Universe, the Atmosphere of Possibilities, that lures humankind upslope.

The catch-22 is this. The Church must morph to survive. Can the Church survive morphing?

This is a conundrum. The reality question is --

How do church members morph their beliefs in the Comprehensible God of the Bible Verse, the Foundation of the Church, to beliefs in the Incomprehensible God of the Universe, the Atmosphere of Possibilities, without destroying the Church?

This is not a pure theological question about the nature of God. For Christians, it is a theological question as slanted by the Christian Religion's perspective of the nature of God.

Theology is not a singular noun. There is no one theology, there are myriad theologies. No person or group can confirm the nature of God. They can but espouse their comprehensions (better stated – conceptualizations) of God's nature.

How difficult will it be to morph our understandings of the nature of God?

Humankind finds butterflies that conform and float effortlessly to be more acceptable than caterpillars that question and struggle mightily. . . does God?

TFB 2. Theology for Beginners?

It occurs to me that the starting point for lay members of the church who desire to morph our belief systems in preparation for morphing the church to follow the Atmosphere of Possibilities to survival, could be a short, basic course in theology. Could the title for such a course be, "Theology for Beginners?" What better research source than the internet?

I offered "Theology for Beginners" to Google, clicked on search and stepped back as 728,000 entries fitting that request rushed to serve me. My repeat of the same title on the altar of the Yahoo search engine was even more overwhelming – 946,000 entries available at the mere click of a mouse.

In the fashion of establishing a geographic point by being blindfolded, twirled three times and aimed at a wall map with a map pin in hand, I randomly clicked on one of the web addresses offered. My reward was instantaneous. An article from a journal on religion was mine for the printing. Its title was, "A Layman's Theology." This promised to be like panning pure gold. . . But as I read the article the nuggets began to shrink to hematite dust. Here is the opening paragraph:

"The layman who proposes to discuss theology is at best presumptuous, if not foolhardy. Theology is the especial province of the clergy and of the faculties of divinity schools. These men are specialists who have devoted years of study and research to the field of religion. They have accumulated knowledge of the nature of God, the meaning of life, and the essentials of faith. They have become well-versed in the Scriptures as "revealed truth," they have discovered what they believe to be the will of God in the affairs of men. They have developed supernatural and superhuman sanctions for other-worldly virtues which should be exemplified in human behavior. They have thus prepared to interpret the human experiences, especially those which perplex the layman."

The article then denigrated the layman as:
…"usually untutored in such matters…it is clear that any layman who undertakes to discuss theological matters speaks only for, and perhaps to, himself. His conception of God, of the meaning of life, and the nature of religion will probably satisfy no other. Especially is this likely when his conceptions rest upon intuition, inspiration or even logic. Such bases completely remove his interpretations from objective demonstration. The layman's theology is hence probably as unsubstantial as that of the clergyman."

(Blog author's note: I couldn't understand the last sentence quoted above. I have searched the entire article before and following the last sentence in the paragraph above to determine why the author rendered such a sentence. I even spent good money to procure a copy of the entire article. I can only conjecture that the author of the article meant to follow the word clergyman with a repeat of these words – "when the clergyman's conceptions rest upon intuition, inspiration or even logic."
Or a second thought: Is the author pegging clergy persons at a pecking position beneath "theologians?")
To study the above quote further I pursue the article further:
". . . it is clear that any layman who undertakes to discuss theological matters speaks only for, and perhaps to, himself. His conception of God, of the meaning of life, and the nature of religion will probably satisfy no other."

My question is – Really? How does this differ from the emanations of "theologians?"

Was this article written during one of the inquisitions?

Not exactly. It was written by a layman, a college professor of religious studies, and published in 1946 by an internationally famous journal of bible and religion.

If this mind-set was typical of the Church in 1946, how did the Church survive the 20th Century?

If we chanced to research too many web sites promoting prejudiced theological views (e.g. "A Layman's Theology") we would skew the course content irreparably. Therefore, random picking of articles from the Google or Yahoo pools, does not appear to be the way to go. We must use these resources selectively rather than randomly.

TFB 3. Designing the Course.

Each unique human has a pinch of response-able spirit that connects him/her with their God (e.g. The Comprehensible God of the Bible Verse, the Climate of Cultures; or, The Incomprehensible God of the Universe, the Atmosphere of Possibilities). I can describe that connection for myself but I cannot define or design it for others.

"Say nothing of my religion," stated Thomas Jefferson. "It's known to my God and myself alone."

As I pause to study this quote, rather than merely "use" it to make a point, I wonder how Thomas Jefferson would have defined the word religion. He states here it is that which secretly connects him to God. We know that Jefferson restructured the New Testament into "The Jefferson Bible" or, "The Life and Morals of Jesus of Nazereth." Was his religion a Judeo-Christian Religion, was it a Christian Religion, a

Christian Faith, a synoptic study of Christ the man? He did remove all supernatural events from his accounting of Christ. I shall leave this study to the reader. Suggested reference:

http://en.wikipedia.org/wiki/Jefferson_Bible

I would pursue a different question here.

What about religion?

The reader will sense that my conceptualization of God has been expanded beyond the box by the metaphor presented by Rolston Holmes, III in "Genes, Genesis and God:"

"God is the atmosphere of possibilities . . . luring the Earthen histories upslope."

It occurred to me that I might explore even further his conceptualizations of - what is religion?

In another Holmes book, "Religious Inquiry – Participation and Detachment," serendipity of serendipities, there is a Chapter 7, "Learning (about) Religion." Readers, please pause a moment to think through this chapter heading – with and without – the "(about)."

There is an old adage, "A word to the wise is sufficient." In this Chapter 7, Holmes gives no "Religion is –" definition, Rather, he states that in learning about religion we must stretch beyond asking, "what is true about our religion?" to asking, "whether our religion is true?" When I stated that we must morph our individual belief systems, I did not state precisely the theological significance of that morphing. I must herein state this significance in "I" terms because I cannot claim it in "we" terms.

Theology is about understanding the nature of God. I cannot confirm the nature of God but I can imagine many human and divine traits that I hope God might have. Since the time when humans first became capable of imagining, human cultures have done this imagining ahead of me.

It is much easier to *image* human traits onto God than to *imagine* the divine traits emanating from God. That is why factious myths and doctrines are so easily contained in "the box" and the atmosphere of possibilities is so difficult to bring into concentrated focus.

Mark Twain reasoned, "Man [the human] is the noblest work of God. Now who found that out?"

The Nature of God is love. Now, how did I find that out?

Fellow humans ahead of me conjectured that God is love and the pinch of spirit in me encourages me to agree. That pinch also encourages me to be response-able to love and hence to God.

The Nature of God is Love. The nature of the human is to be response-able to God. This is faith.

Our families and cultures share with us the templates of God and of love on which our response-able pinches of spirit build our faiths. This is how we "come by" the Faith of Our Fathers. How can I, when I arrive at the "the age of reason," choose my belief system when I already have it?

Please permit me to return to the article "A Layman's Theology" presented in the previous blog. I find described there a prevalent paradigm of theology that is a serious contributor to the need to morph the church.

"...it is clear that any layman who undertakes to discuss theological matters speaks only for, and perhaps to, himself. His conception of God, of the meaning of life, and the nature of religion will probably satisfy no other. Especially is this likely when his conceptions rest upon intuition, inspiration or even logic. Such bases completely remove his interpretations from objective demonstration."

The author of "A Layman's Theology" states that a layperson's theological observations are at risk when his/her conceptions rest upon "intuition, inspiration, or even logic." However, he is apparently willing for his readers to base their conceptions on the "intuition, inspiration, and even logic" of previous or present scholars (pre-

Biblical, Biblical, post-Biblical) whose declinations he pronounces acceptable to God.

What if some of the Biblical conceptions from previous cultures are proven unworthy of "intuition, inspiration, or even logic?"

Chosen people? A wrathful God? Death to all first born Egyptians? Factious doctrines and fictitious miracles?

The church is the preeminent institution undergirding individuals and families within the Christian Religion and Culture. When the church clings to such concepts as above, does this impose inhibitions on adherents striving to release their belief systems beyond the box to explore the Incomprehensible God of the Universe, the Atmosphere of Possibilities?

"A Layman's Theology?" -- "Theology for Beginners?"

Perhaps better that we seek a Theology for the Uninhibited? When the church inhibits the intuition, inspiration and logic of its members by forcing on them the Comprehensible God of the Bible Verse, the Climate of Cultures, their faith is compromised.

TFB 4. Proclaiming Faith – Practicing Manipulation.

Who am I to claim that humans proclaim faith but practice manipulation? I can claim it because I am so accomplished at it.

I have recently finished Eckhart Tolle's book "A New World." I have some difficulty pinning down a name for the inner-self Tolle encourages us to search out. I believe it is "awakened consciousness." It appears to me that I have labeled my consciousness; "a pinch of spirit," a term I picked up long ago by reading Toynbee. Again, I'm not sure but I think that the ages-old term, God, that expresses what I want my pinch of spirit to be response-able to, is something Tolle likens to "the presence," or maybe "the source."

Being response-able to God is faith. When I am not response-able (faithful) to God because I am not sufficiently responsible to my inner-self and to other humans (known or unknown) I am being manipulative. This is not the real inner me, of course, it is my ego, my manipulative self.

How did I come by this manipulative self, this ego? I came by it quite naturally. I observed what worked in life for others and adapted it to my personal capabilities.

How did I come to church membership at age 12? I became a member of the church because of the family and the culture in which I developed. I was told that if I accepted certain beliefs, presented to me by family, church, culture and the Bible, I could be capable of comprehending God to the degree that I would be eligible for membership in the church, a group of believers. Every hour of any day of my life I am thankful for that comprehension and that membership.

In accepting membership was I suddenly morphed into a human who shed ego completely and became response-able totally? Of course not. Did I believe I was "saved"TO or FOR something? How could I when, at age 12, I was not even sure what being "saved" meant.

Was I "born again?" What could this mean to a 12 year old trying to figure out his first birth?

However, there was a bright side. As I looked at life around me, I could cite innumerable, catastrophic evils I was saved FROM - because I became a member of the Church of the Comprehensible God of the Bible Verse.

Then, why am I so strenuous, creating all these rambling blogs about morphing the church? Why? Because the church (that's us) has too long permitted the presentation of factious myths and doctrines to its collected members, e.g. "Jesus Christ, and hence Christ's Church, is the only way to 'salvation.' The Scriptures are the inerrant Word of God." Such dogmas not only permit, rather they encourage, our collective egos to proclaim faith while practicing manipulation.

I want the church to help me compromise my ego rather than my faith so that within the Atmosphere of Possibilities a morphed me can help a morphed church expand the Kindom of God.

TFB 5. A Dilemma.

Here I pause to face a dilemma. The Comprehensible God of the Bible Verse is the foundation of a church in which many members are coming to recognize that the human has over-comprehended God to the point of distortion. Humankind, in the millennia before there was a church, distorted the supernatural time after time to comprehend (then develop) various templates of the divine (e.g. pagan gods) that the human hoped could somehow extend the temporal, human life into an eternal, spiritual life.

At a point in religious history a small tribe of humans condensed the comprehension of various templates of many gods to a one God template. Their culture retained, as an oral tradition, this multi-century event as transpiring within the lifetime of one individual human, Abram.

Per the Biblical account Abram was chosen by God, at age 75, to lead this specific people to a land God promised Abram. This small faction of the earth's population developed a factious oral history of this Comprehensible God having conversations with Abram and directing the movements of this people - directing them so lovingly and specifically, per their over-comprehensions, that they came to consider themselves "chosen."

This is where human religious practices lose their way. It is when I consider myself chosen that I proclaim faith but practice manipulation. My ego over-comprehends my relationship with Comprehensible God and manipulation distorts my response-able faith.

What do I mean when I state, or admit, that I over-comprehend God? (I would suggest that "admit" is the more accurate term because many persons today are coming to consider over-comprehending outside the limits of healthy religious practice.)

If my comprehension of God has me being more faithful than others, or has God choosing me over others, this is a comprehension that takes me beyond the line of healthy response-ableness.

If Abram's followers were a chosen people or if the theologians described in "A Layman's Theology" (TFB 2.) thought they comprehended "revealed truths. . . and the will of God" per the following quote, were both of these examples of truth or of over-comprehension?

"They have accumulated knowledge of the nature of God, the meaning of life, and the essentials of faith. They have become well-versed in the Scriptures as "revealed truth," they have discovered what they believe to be the will of God in the affairs of men."

Have the Scriptures derived from previous cultures that over-comprehended their template of God?

Additionally:

Do we strive to make the God of the Bible Verse Comprehensible because we over-comprehend these Scriptures to be "revealed truth and the inerrant Word of God?"

TFB 6. Scriptures – Culturally derived? Divinely revealed?

Have the Scriptures derived from previous cultures that over-comprehended their God?

A strange thing happened on the way to theology. If theology is a study of the nature of God and religious belief why don't theologians start their study with primitive humans who found The Divinity within their Universe to be Incomprehensible? Why do theologians bypass thousands of years of Incomprehensibility and start their academic, theological sparring at that point where Divinity has been rendered Comprehensible – and, unfortunately, Over-Comprehensible – in the Judeo-Christian Scriptures?

The earliest humans survived through instinctual actions, augmented by sensory reactions, while intelligence was developing very gradually to become an ever more prominent factor within survival. Although comprehension of reality developed concurrently with intelligence, over-comprehensions still permitted aberrant imaginations of the unreal and surreal.

Over-comprehension produced a spirit for every danger, disease, animal, dark corner, eclipse, or weather phenomenon; and supplied a god for every seasonal, celestial, physiological, pathological or emotional change.

But then came a turning. The spirits became more manageable and the number of gods began to shrink. To a small faction of humanity The One God became more and more Comprehensible as the Creator of the heavens and the earth and all of life. But here let us pause.

Humans did the best they could to comprehend that which they were not capable of comprehending. How could they be capable? **Their only basis for their understanding the nature of God was to image human traits onto God and imagine super-human traits emanating from God.** They over-comprehended. Advanced as we may consider ourselves, we've been doing it ever since.

Per the Bible:

Early on this God created a man and a woman. A bit later, in a second account of this same event, this same God does "The Original Extreme Makeover." In this makeover God made the man from dust first and later the woman from one of the man's ribs. How can one explain these contradictory stories? One cannot. One can only identify them for what they are – the first accounts of biblical over-comprehension. They are also another first – Exhibit A. in disputation of the inerrancy of the Bible.

Word upon word and book upon book have been written to present over-comprehensions of God and to establish the Scriptures as Revealed and Inerrant.

In contradistinction word upon word and book upon book have been written to refute these over-comprehensions and disestablish the Scriptures as revealed and inerrant.

This blog series won't make any systematic effort to analyze specifics within the Scriptures to establish or disestablish that the Scriptures are or are not revealed and inerrant. Such analyses by competent scholars are available and should be studied. Each member of the church must weigh the evidence and then hold to that belief system which answers for them this question -

How does the church morph its beliefs from the Comprehensible God of the Bible Verse, the climate of cultures, to the Incomprehensible God of the Universe, the atmosphere of possibilities – to survive?

TFB 7. From Over-Comprehension to Over-Inhibition

In a previous series of blogs I offered the conclusion that church members, and in turn the church, must think beyond the box in order to explore the Atmosphere of Possibilities* that could empower the church to morph and hence survive.

This box has come to the church through thousands of years of a climate of cultures that developed the oral and written ABCs filling the box:

A. Factious Fundamentals and Doctrines.

B. Embellished Stories and Myths.

C. Outmoded Knowledge and Cultures.

Much within the box is sound, true and essential to response-able beliefs. (Because members have practiced it the church has survived all these centuries.) But in the current climate much within the box is over-comprehended (factious and fictitious) and weakening to belief systems. (Because of this members must think beyond the box for the church to survive.)

Many members **and nonmembers** who would morph their personal belief systems, and the collective beliefs of the church, find that the contents of the box inhibit their exploration of the Atmosphere of Possibilities. Much that the church claims to be revealed truth and the inerrant word of God inhibits rather than enhances their exploration.

Who, then, are the uninhibited? The Uninhibited are those persons not inhibited by the contents of the box that we are to think beyond to morph our belief systems and the teachings of the church so that it can survive.

I believe that Jesus, the Ultimately Response-Able Steward, would give permission to add this beatitude to his list: Blessed are the Uninhibited for they shall recognize the Atmosphere of Possibilities.

*What is the Atmosphere of Possibilities? This is a metaphor that Holmes Rolston III uses in his book, "Genes, Genesis and God, Their Origins in Natural and Human History," to describe the Nature of the Incomprehensible God of the Universe as the Atmosphere of Possibilities.

TFB 8. Why Are We Inhibited?

From its genesis religion has been based on beliefs that elevated the minds of its adherents away from the mundane, physical human to the stimulating, metaphysical divine (eventually termed God). Out of this transference grew the histories, stories, myths, miracles, imaginations, even hallucinations that carried forward from BCE (Before the Common Era) into the CE (Common Era). Jesus was born and his life became (deservedly) the pivotal point defining the two eras. The life of Jesus so moved many humans searching for the stimulating metaphysical that they conveyed on him the title Christ to emphasize his powers to make this connection between the mundane human and the stimulating metaphysical.

Out of this comprehension of Christ as a connection grew the church as an institutional connector.

Intelligence carries with it the ability to comprehend. In an earlier blog I offered the theory that the human has an innate ability to over-comprehend. This is different from imagine. Normally a true imagination does not have a rational basis. Over-comprehension can be an over-expansion of plausibility.

As the church expanded its comprehension of Christ it was very natural that these comprehensions be based on authenticity beyond the human mind. Hence the earlier blog quote that these comprehensions were of, "revealed truth and the will of God in the affairs of men."

There arose differences of levels of comprehension within the church, even of what was comprehensible. This led to the Councils of the early centuries. A study of these councils and a comparative review of our current church assemblies lend support to the observation that life forms are evolving at a rate faster than human nature.

Back to the Councils. After huge fights over what to comprehend, and at what level to comprehend it, there was always the inherent danger that those who lost would over-comprehend (or under-comprehend) it to suit their position. It is remarkable that any degree of unanimity arose from these encounters, but not remarkable that so much discord exists, and appears to be growing almost 2,000 years later.

This explains my earlier statement that there is much material in the boxes we must think beyond if we and the church are to morph our belief systems sufficiently to effect survival of the church.

As these blogs have developed there are continuing examples of these over-comprehensions and the contents of the box. In my research I have come upon many most interesting articles on all sides of this dilemma and here I will pause to share an excellent one of them at some length.

One doesn't tip-toe very far into the history of the Christian Church until one finds oneself in Nicea, now Iznik on Lake Iznik in Turkey, in the year 325 CE (A.D.). The material which follows is condensed from an article on the Council of Nicea found at the following website:

http://stphilipscathedral.org/pdf/021107.pdf

Or by going to Google: "Cathedral Times; Can a Non-Biblical Word be Orthodox? February 11, 2007."

A new Roman Emperor, Constantine, had received as a vision a sign of Jesus Christ before a critical battle at the Milivan Bridge on the Tiber River. The Romans won the battle and the western world changed when Constantine then accepted Christianity.

Constantine noticed that Christianity was not monolithic. Strife concerned the divine nature of Jesus Christ. Was Christ fully divine or not? Constantine called for a Council of the Church to settle this inconsistency in Nicea in 325.

At Nicea, the Bishop of Alexandria represented the orthodox view that Jesus Christ, the Word, was truly God. The bishop and his successor, Athanasius, used the phrase **"Homo-ousios"** meaning "of the same substance" to refer to Jesus Christ. Jesus Christ, though the "Son" of God, was of the same substance as the Father; thus, Jesus Christ was fully divine.

However, "homo-ousios" was not a biblical term and could not be found in the Bible in order to establish a precedent.

Also out of Alexandria came the opponent Arius, a handsome and musical man who carried a popular counter sentiment. Arius argued not only that **"homo-ousios"** was unbiblical, but that the Bible (at Proverbs 8:22) spoke of divine wisdom (the "word") as created. If the word was created, the word must not be fully divine. Arius also proclaimed that because Jesus was clearly the "Son" of God, surely "there was a time when he was not." A son, went the argument, surely comes from a father, the father must exist first. Arius claimed that there was only one God, God the Father, and Jesus was God's Son; but Jesus was not God.

Arius preferred the Greek phrase **"homoi-ousios."** Does the word "homoi-ousios" look like the word "homo-ousios?" Yes, of course it does. But the words are different. There is one letter different. It is the letter "i." In Greek that letter is "iota."

(Blog Editor note: Here the reader might like to take a break and Google two terms; "not one iota of difference," and the term, "an iota of difference.")

Arius preferred the term **"homoi-ousios"** because it means "of a similar substance." If Jesus was the "Son" of God, argued Arius, then

Jesus was "of a similar substance" as God the Father, but Jesus was not "of the same substance" as God the Father.

Finally taking a cue from the former creed of Eusebius of Caesarea, the Council of Nicea decided for **"homo-ousios."** That is why the Nicene Creed says "of one being with the Father." The word for "being" is "ousios," "substance," Hence that final word, homoousios is not exactly a biblical word.

Even then, the Nicene Creed was not exactly the final word, either. The political tides (Blog Editor's Note: the comprehensions, the over-comprehensions, the under-comprehensions) went back and forth, depending upon who was Roman emperor, depending on whose voice was loudest at the time. The followers of Arius became quite influential; and Athanasius himself was exiled from Alexandria on five different occasions! The difference came to be represented as one iota, the English letter "i." That letter was the difference between saying that Jesus was merely like the being of the Father, or saying that Jesus was of the same being as the Father. Orthodox Christianity, over time, became convinced that Jesus, was indeed, fully part of the Godhead, of the same being as the Father. The phrase "of the same being" is not in the Bible, but it is orthodox. We proclaim it every Sunday. Ω

This blogger thanks the author of the above-quoted article for this most lucid explanation of "homo-ousios" and "homoi-ousios."

I shall not presume to interpret the intent of the author. I can only report what the well-written article says to me; as I struggle to explain, within this specific blog: **"Why Are We Inhibited?"**

There is all the difference between winning a discourse through "explaining" and through "inhibiting." At the Council of Nicea words of explanation were one thing, but words from the Sacred Scriptures were another. It made an iota of difference. Words that convey "revealed truth" are "inerrant" and authentic. What if a word cannot be found in the Bible to say what we want to say? Are we then "inhibited?" Is it "authentic" to make up a word and declare it "orthodox?"

But, I have wandered into **nit-picking!** I shall change the question: **"Why Am I Inhibited?"**

Why am I inhibited by The Nicene Creed that has me say, "of one substance with the Father," when I believe the Trinity to be an over-comprehension?

Why am I inhibited by the Apostles' Creed that has me say, "Christ descended into hell?" when the concept "hell" doesn't nurture my response-able faith that God is love?

No! -- **"Why am I inhibited?"** is a negative and insecure approach.

Finally -- I think I've got it. How might we employ a 21st Century Beatitude in morphing the church?

Blessed are the Uninhibited for they shall recognize the Atmosphere of Possibilities.

TFTU 9. Theology For The Uninhibited.

Yes, the headings of the blogs in this series have changed from TFB (Theology for Beginners) to TFTU (Theology For The Uninhibited). I'll leave the numbering sequence as is.

I realize that the term "Uninhibited" carries with it connotations that may be misinterpreted. However, my thesis is that many of the factors hampering the church are inhibitions (as part of the contents of the box). This gives validity to applying a countering identification, "Uninhibited," to those who would morph the church. To explain this succinctly I shall insert an earlier quote that I find helpful:

"To be truly creative one must break mental sets and think beyond reality."   Jay Yanoff

After spending some hours studying the brouhaha at the Council of Nicea, plus innumerable hours attending PCUSA meetings of Presbytery, Synod and General Assembly, I can understand why the church would not be ecstatic about submitting its plethora of mental sets to various group processes. Task forces, assemblies, committees, teleconferences, and questionnaires ad infinitum would bankrupt the physical, fiscal and spiritual resources of the entire church with little to show for the effort.

A thought occurs to me. Let's take another look at the words "homo-ousios" and "homoi-ousios."

1. "homo" in the Greek means "same," as in "homogenized" milk; "ousios" in the Greek means "substance" or "being.

"homoi" (note the additional iota) in the Greek means

"similar" or "like;" and again "ousios means "substance" or "being."

Thus we have two Greek words: "homoousios" meaning "of the same substance," and "homoiousios" meaning "of like (or similar) substance."

At the Council of Nicea the struggle was whether God and Christ were homoousios or homoiousios. (I don't mean to be flippant to God or disrespectful to Christ but in my Google search I came upon a web site with a sermon titled, "Homoousios? Homoiousios? Who Cares?" It was a good sermon. It almost lived up to its title.)

What if my pinch of spirit and your pinch of spirit were homoiousios (as in our uniquely similar but different DNA markings)? What if Jesus had a DNA marking similar but different (of course) from each of ours? Here is the heretical, what if shocker. "What if" Jesus also had a pinch of homoiousios spirit like yours or mine? **Here, of course, the comparison ends because he made his pinch ultimately response-able and we will barely use ours.**

I must admit that this exercise has me sitting here at my computer chuckling. Not as a smart aleck or a delusional extrovert, but as an "Uninhibited." As an Uninhibited pondering how livid some of my peers reading this must be with this "apostate blogger" risking the intricate circuitry of his trusty Macintosh to wrathful destruction by the Trinitarian God discovered (developed?) at Nicea in 325 CE.

TFTU 10. Does The Inerrant Inhibit?

Does the inerrant (incapable of being wrong) inhibit? The non-specific answer to this non-specific question is – Yes!

Here is the question phrased more fully:

In using its Inerrant Scriptures as a basis for nurturing and directing its members, does the Christian Religion (the Church) restrict the beings, as well as direct the beliefs, of its adherents to a comprehensible cultural climate of expectations rather than an incomprehensible atmosphere of possibilities?

My answer is an emphatic, **YES!**

It has taken me long years and many experiences to attain the courage, within my attempts at response-ableness to the Incomprehensible God of the Universe and my struggles toward responsibility to the comprehensible human needs of the Earth, to consider morphing my belief system from comprehensible expectations to incomprehensible possibilities.

It has taken the church long centuries and countless innocent-errancies to discover the imperative that it must morph to survive.

(Glossary: **innocent-errancy** – a coined term to express the state of believing errant information innocently because it is the best explanation currently available. e.g. The world is flat (1491), the Biblical creation stories, the early concept that the Sun rotated around the Earth.)

See Glossary, page 189.

In blog TFTU 8, the process of establishing a monolithic church through long weeks at the Council of Nicea, 325 CE, was described as utilizing negative inhibition more than positive explanation to accomplish persuasion. When explanation failed, inhibition was applied.

An example of the use of the term innocent-errancy as an inhibition:

At Nicea, when rational discourse failed to find a way to document that God and Jesus were of one substance through some definitive word in the inerrant Scripture, the faction of Athanasius presented the word homoousios meaning of one substance and the followers of Arius presented the word homoiousios meaning of similar substance. The Council accepted the word homoousios and thus started morphing the One, Unpleasant God of the Old Testament into the Kinder-Gentler, Tripartite God of the New Testament.

Surely if a small council of 318 bishops meeting in Nicea in 325 CE from May 20 to August 25 could bring their pinches of spirit to bear on the first iota in homoiousios and thereby morph the Church's God from Yahweh to the Trinity, we of the 21st Century can use our millions of pinches to morph the church from the Comprehensible God of the Bible Verse, the Climate of Cultures, to the Incomprehensible God of the Universe, the Atmosphere of Possibilities.

TFTU 11. How to Create an Innocent-Errancy

Since its beginnings the Church has faced the task of reviewing oral and written materials from many factions within or without the Church for purposes of acceptance or rejection. Such material from factions is properly labeled factious material. Factious describes materials coming from factions, i.e. a description of the source of materials. The word sounds like fictitious but the meanings are very different. Fictitious describes imaginary, false or made up material, i.e. a description of the nature of materials.

Thus, at Nicea for example, the factions of Arius and of Athanasius presented factious material. Both stated that Jesus was the son of God. Athanasius stated that God and Jesus were of the same substance and hence God and Jesus were both God. Arius stated that God and Jesus were only of similar substances and hence Jesus could not be God.

Since the claims were diametric both could not be true. Therefore the Council took as its mission of the moment the task of deciding which factious claim was true. Councils being human by make-up and by nature, no doubt many of those present defined the mission of the council as deciding which claim was fictitious.

Apparently no one, way in the back of the group, raised a hand and asked, "Honorable Presiding Bishop, since God is, by all rational accounts, an incomprehensible spirit, what comprehensible substance is God made of? Since Jesus was of comprehensible substance, what pray tell, is this Council all about? I move that this Council adjourn and spare the Christian Faith untold centuries of Trinitarian dysfunction."

The motion was not made and over its centuries since, the Church has dealt with much factious material. Some it rejected. Some it placed in its Box as the Bible, The Sacred Scripture, The Primary Inerrant Word. Other secondary materials such as creeds, confessions, tenets, etc. made it into some boxes of some factions of the church and not others. Apparently it was difficult for our forefathers to decide what was primary, sacred and revealed, and what was secondary, inspired and recorded.

When factious material did not fit the template of the Bible, not to worry, just add one tiny iota to homoousios, create homoiousios, debate a few weeks but then adopt homoousios anyway. Presto - the solution is an Innocent Errancy that morphs Yahweh to the God in Three Persons.

And with that proclamation of faith through the practice of manipulation the Council of Nicea adjourned on the 25th day of August, 325 CE.

TFTU 12. A Detour Into Atheism

After using several blogs to present the expansion of Innocent-Errancies at Nicea in 325 CE, I was going to explore the difference between conceptualizations and innocent-errancies. The title of the blog was to be, "My Very Own Conceptualization." I'll save the title and come back to it later.

In the meantime please come with me on an exploration of atheism. First some definitions:

Gnosticism – noun - a prominent heretical movement of the 2nd Century Christian Church, partly of pre Christian origin, Gnostic doctrine taught that the world was created and ruled by a lesser divinity, the demiurge, and that Christ was an emissary of the remote supreme divine being - esoteric knowledge (gnosis) of whom enabled the redemption of the human spirit.

Gnostic – noun - an adherent of Gnosticism.

Agnostic – noun - a person who believes that nothing is known or can be known of the existence or nature of God or anything beyond material phenomena; a person who claims neither faith nor disbelief in God.

deism – noun – belief in the existence of a supreme being, specifically a creator who does not intervene in the universe. The term is used chiefly as an intellectual movement in the 17th and 18th centuries that accepted the existence of a creator on the basis of reason but rejected belief in a supernatural deity who interacts with humankind. Compare with THEISM.

theism – noun – belief in the existence of a god or gods, esp. belief in one god as creator of the universe, intervening in it and sustaining a personal relation to "his" Creatures. Compare with DEISM.

atheism – noun – the theory or belief that God does not exist.

atheist – noun – one who subscribes to the theory of atheism.

It was Constantine and the Council of Nicea that tried to render the church powerful by developing a monolithic comprehension of God. Then, over following centuries, the church put that comprehension into comprehensible written form, a canon, the Bible. To authenticate this written comprehension the church labeled it the "Word of God" and declared it "Inerrant."

As I have tried to think beyond the box of ABCs to compare the Comprehensible God of the Bible Verse, The Climate of Cultures, to the Incomprehensible God of the Universe, the Atmosphere of Possibilities, I realize that my use of the word Incomprehensible is an invitation to those who would sweep me aside as an agnostic. I certainly do not subscribe to Gnosticism. Nor do I match the definition of agnostic as given above. Neither does the fact that I find God Incomprehensible deny me belief in God or define God as non-existent. I find string theory physics incomprehensible, but - who knows? Could it be true?

Two weeks ago I took a vacation from blogging and set out to explore seriously that which is labeled atheism. I went to the search engines of the Web for a definition. It seems that there are varieties of atheists. "Strong" atheists believe there is no god or gods. "Weak" or "implicit" atheists stand against theism, wherein the god intervenes in human affairs. My readings of several positions brought me to the conclusion that I should find an author who based his/her rationale on what is an objective study of religion as well as science. Note that I did not use the term objective analysis, I used the term objective study.

One cannot analyze religion. One can analyze science. But I find it much too delimiting to declare that the struggle is between religion and science. The ultimate struggle is not about what does or does not exist, it is about what the human is capable of comprehending. After reviewing several works on the subject I settled on the 2006 book by Richard Dawkins, THE GOD DELUSION, published by Houghton-Mifflin Company, Boston. I vowed that I would not touch this blog until I had completed a reading and study of the book. And now I have kept the vow.

It may not surprise the readership of this blog that Dawkins and I agree on many of the foibles and shortcomings of religion. It certainly should not surprise the readership that I wandered in a total daze through the fantastic knowledge of science that Dawkins presents. I hope that it will not surprise the reader that Dawkins and I parted at the final page of his excellently presented thesis with open minds, but each with the same belief system that he had entered it.

Chapter 10. of Dawkins' book is titled, "A Much Needed Gap?" This is of course a sympathetic, but yet not acceptable to Dawkins, premise that the human needs the comfort of a God delusion for happiness and stability. Here is how Dawkins puts it on page 352 under the subtitle:

"CONSOLATION

It is time to face up to the important role that God plays in consoling us; and the humanitarian challenge, if he does not exist, to put something in his place. Many people who concede that God probably doesn't exist, and that he is not necessary for mortality, still come back with what they often regard as a trump card: the alleged psychological or emotional *need* for a god. If you take religion away, people truculently ask, what are we going to put in its place? What do you have to offer the dying patients, the weeping bereaved, the lonely Eleanor Rigby's for whom God is their only friend?"

Observation 1. I am amazed to find Dawkins describing the God he does not believe in as the cultural, anthropomorphic "he." Could this be evidence that Dawkins' God delusion is of the Comprehensible God trapped in the ABCs box and not the Incomprehensible God of the Universe, the Atmosphere of Possibilities?

Observation 2. Dawkins goes on to quote from D. C. Dennett (2006 *Breaking the Spell: Religion as a Natural Phenomenon.* London: Viking). Dennett makes the distinction between believing in God and belief in belief, even if the belief itself is false. Dawkins concurs with Dennett as expressed in the following quote:

"The faithful are encouraged to *profess* belief, whether they are convinced by it or not. Maybe if you repeat something often enough, you will succeed in convincing yourself of its truth. I think we all know people who enjoy the idea of religious faith and resent attacks on it, while reluctantly admitting that they don't have it themselves."

My observation: This blogger sees "belief in belief" as one of the over-comprehensions (see glossary for **ABCs**) which religion has pushed onto adherents in an attempt to compress Incomprehensible God to Comprehensible.

Observation 3. I found what, to me, was the summary statement of Dawkins' 374 page book in the middle of page 360:

"There is something infantile in the presumption that somebody else (parents in the case of children, God in the case of adults) has a responsibility to give your life meaning and point."

My response: If anti-infantilism is the basis (or essence) of atheism, where does the atheist find the mature love responsible for stewardship of the earth and survival relationships within humanity?

To conclude my detour to atheism I return to a previous statement in this blog, TFTU 12:

But I find it much too delimiting to declare that the struggle is between religion and science. The ultimate struggle is not about what does or does not exist, it is about what the human is capable of comprehending.

I make a limited claim of my capability to comprehend some science. I make two claims re my comprehension of religion – 1. God is love. 2. God is Incomprehensible.

TFTU 13. My Very Own Conceptualization

Examples of the terms innocent-errancy and conceptualization:

There was absolutely no way to settle the Nicean controversy over the innocent-errancy that Jesus Christ and God are of the same substance, or of a similar substance. Jesus had being (substance). Does spirit God have being (substance)? There is absolutely no way that I can prove my conceptualization that there is a Pinch of God's Spirit having no substance in my body that does have substance. Neither statement is provable.

I am not a deist. I do not believe that God created the universe(s) and went to the shade. Nor am I a theist. I do not believe that God sits in the shade numbering the decreasing hairs of my head or is out there trying to find me a parking place at the shopping center. I conceptualize God as the Incomprehensible Atmosphere of Possibilities.

If God is incomprehensible, why should I struggle with the innocent-errancies (eg. deist vs. theist, homoousios vs. homoiousios) of theologians when I can dream up tons of the same on my own?

Neither do I want my beliefs to be infantile.

Dawkins: "There is something infantile in the presumption that somebody else (parents in the case of children, God in the case of adults) has a responsibility to give your life meaning and point."

Does this infer one should advocate orphanhood or atheism on the presumption that one has no need for support on the "meaning or point" in ones life?

What are the meaning and point of my life ? I would define mine this way: I want to be response-able to something beyond me so that I can live responsibly amongst the humanity here with me.

Science proposes particles of matter and non-matter that most of us cannot comprehend. Religion proposes miracles and myths of biogenesis and supernatural genesis of "same" and "similar" matter that are counter to comprehension of the natural.

So what does this invisible speck in the Universe, me, propose?

"I believe that the Incomprehensible God of the Universe is an Atmosphere of Possibilities within which the human can be a response-able steward to and for the Incomprehensible God - and responsible to and with all of humanity, including self."

This is not a theological statement. It is my very own ultimate-survival, conceptualization and it gets me by from one day to the next.

Conclusion: One person's conceptualization may be termed an innocent-errancy by others and visa-versa.

TFTU 14. A Paradox Beyond the Box

In how many ways have I attempted to present that the human cannot comprehend God? Innocent-errancies and the ABCs of the Box are ways humans contrive to **comprehend** God. Such contriving within our various cultural climates has resulted in *conceptualizations* of God, not *comprehensions*. Humans have contrived to reduce the Incomprehensible God of the Universe, the Atmosphere of Possibilities, to the Comprehensible God of the Book (e.g. Bible) Verse, the Climate of Cultures.

Within the climate of cultures, one must realize that theologians as well as non-theologians issue assumptions and conceptualizations not truths and comprehensions.

Those who would study the nature of God (theology) too often start with a study of the boxed God, the Comprehensible God of the Book Verse, rather than the beyond the box God, the Incomprehensible God of the Universe.

Please note: this diversionary use of the term "Book Verse" takes me beyond my valid frame of Judeo-Christian reference, "Bible Verse," for a brief moment merely to demonstrate the width and complexity of the term theology.

My belief system, our belief systems, are not based on comprehensions of the nature of God. They are based on conceptualizations of the nature of God. My conceptualizations have gradually morphed to dare me to venture beyond the inhibitions that I find within the climate of the church to an uninhibited atmosphere of possibilities.

Remember way back when, in this blog series, We discovered the admonition: "The Church must change or it will die." We softened it to: "The Church must morph to survive." I offered that we as members of the Church must morph our individual belief systems so that the communal belief system of the Church could morph.

Here we arrive again at a serious Catch-22. Can the church survive its adherents morphing their belief systems? Put in the opposite manner – can church members morph their beliefs without institutional – encouragement? endorsement? permission?

My primal logic is this – if the Church could survive the Nicean Experience, contributing to morphing the   Unpleasant Yahweh to the Kinder/Gentler God in Three Persons, then exist through some contentious centuries since, it surely can survive the morphing of its human adherents in these more enlightened times.

TFTU 15. I Can, Yes I Can.

I can morph my belief system, and I am. I can't tell you the precise moment I started, but the process is underway. It is difficult to chronicle precisely the development, and then the morphing, of ones belief system.

Your process will be entirely different from mine, so this is not a "how to" testimonial for others to follow. It is merely a reassurance that if I can do it anybody can.

To present a logical sequence of the process I outline here the chronology of life's stages - as I see them.

Stage I. Childhood.
Phase1. Prior to "Age of Reason." About age 12.
Phase 2. Up to driving age.

Stage II. Almost Adulthood.
Phase 1. From driving age to self-sustaining age.
Stage III. Adulthood.
Phase 1. Inhibited Self-Sustainment.
Phase 2. Uninhibited Self-Sustainment.

Here listed are a few of the precepts in my belief system as they have appeared and now appear in the phases of my life :

During Childhood, Phase 1:
Love, safety, security, (Early on) Santa Claus, Easter Bunny, Tooth Fairy, Nursery Rhymes, Bedtime Stories, Select Bible Stories, (Later) Multiplication Tables. God is theist, Jesus loves me (my culture and the Bible tell me so).

During Childhood, Phase 2:
Love, safety, security, Select Bible Stories, Biblical Myths and Miracles, Biblical and Other guides to moral stability, A mostly empty ABCs of Religion Box, Expanding Mathematics, Life skills. God is theist and deist, Jesus is my big brother (the Bible, the culture and the church tell me so).

During Almost Adulthood, Phase 1:

Love, safety, security, Lessening study of select Bible Stories, Expanding study of Biblical Myths and Miracles, Expanding study of Biblical and other guides to moral stability, A fuller ABCs of Religion Box, Applying mathematics, Interest in physics of the Universe, more life skills, vocational knowledge. God is comprehensible, Jesus is the Christ (the Bible, the church and my culture tell me so).

During Adulthood, Phase 1.
Love, safety, security, Questioning Biblical Myths and Miracles, Better understanding of Biblical and other guides to moral stability, Questioning the ABCs of Religion Box, Shrinking mathematics, Physics of the Universe becoming difficult to understand, life skills utilized, vocational experience. God is comprehensible, Christ is God Incarnate (the Bible, the church, my culture and external inhibitory pressures tell me so).

During Adulthood, Phase 2.
Love, safety, security, Abandoning Biblical Myths and Miracles, Better utilization of Biblical and other guides to moral stability, Thinking beyond the ABCs of Religion Box, Leaving mathematics to others, Physics of the Universe totally incomprehensible, life skills shared, vocational fulfillment, God is the Incomprehensible God of the Universe, the Atmosphere of Possibilities, Jesus was the ultimate response-able person (my response-able, uninhibited self tells me so).

Now that you have read the precepts as a whole, I suggest that you start at the first phase, choose each precept in turn as it first appears and then follow its changes (if any) to the final phase in which it appears.

As I review this schema of life, I am reminded of an earlier quote of Richard Dawkins on the life process:

"There is something infantile in the presumption that somebody else (parents in the case of children, God in the case of adults) has a responsibility to give your life meaning and point."

My earlier response to this quote was:

"What are the meaning and point of my life? I would define mine this way: I want to be response-able to something beyond me so that I can live responsibly amongst the humanity here with me."

At this point I would add that being response-able to God adds this meaning and point to our lives - the ability to stretch rather than shrink.

TFTU 16. Morphing – How Does Transition Begin?

The reader may remember that I concluded TFTU 13. "My Very Own Conceptualization," with a statement that could be interpreted as a belief statement by some or as an Innocent Errancy by others.

Just because we members, or the church for that matter, pronounce a statement to be a belief does not preclude the possibility that it might be errant, innocently or otherwise.

Here again is the statement:

"I believe that the Incomprehensible God of the Universe is an Atmosphere of Possibilities within which the human can be a response-able steward to and for the Incomprehensible God - and responsible to and with all of humanity, including self."

This is not intended to be a theological statement. It is my *conceptualization* of being response-able to God. It is not a *comprehension* of what we must believe to be saved - **someday**. It is my very own conceptualization for a joyous survival in an atmosphere of possibilities, that gets me by - in **these days** - to whatever follows.

I have come to be response-able to the Incomprehensible God of Possibilities rather than a Comprehensible God of Inhibitions.

I desire to be responsible to all of humanity alongside fellow humans who search for compassionate possibilities rather than outmoded inhibitions. Therefore I shall describe the morphing of my belief system as a transition from inhibitions to possibilities.

I do not profess to be a Biblical Scholar or Authority.

I have read and I do read the Bible as a mostly-sound guide for living derived from previous times and cultures. One cannot read very far into the Bible before one faces the inhibiting dilemma that these writings given as fact do not match the hoped for world that we have come to describe as the **Kindom** of God

I resist accepting the Bible as inerrant nor as the Word of God, lest I be tempted to idolize it. To me it is the words of men/women who were expressing their conceptualizations of that they deemed to be the Comprehensible God of their cultures and times.

As it was acceptable for persons in Biblical times to express their conceptualizations it is acceptable for persons in these cultural, and more enlightened physical-science, times to express their conceptualizations. This does not infer that expanded knowledge of the natural gives greater current insights into the supernatural. Because we know more about a comprehensible creation does not mean we know more about the incomprehensible creator, although we do possess an entirely different basis on which to conceptualize.

A few paragraphs ago I promised to: "describe the morphing of my belief system as a transition from inhibitions to possibilities." And here I start.

My belief system started when I was first touched and loved. It began verbally when I first heard this song:

Jesus loves me! this I know,
For the Bible tells me so.
Little ones to Him belong;
They are weak but He is strong.

Yes, Jesus loves me!
Yes, Jesus loves me!
Yes, Jesus loves me!
The Bible tells me so.

I did not have to go to Wikipedia to find these lyrics. I know them. They are rote – set like words on stone in my cerebral cortex.

(Once a young student asked Karl Barth if he could sum up what was most important about his life's work and theology in just a few words. The question was posed even with gasps from the audience. Barth just thought for a moment and then smiled, "Yes, in the words of a song my mother used to sing me, 'Jesus loves me, this I know, for the Bible tells me so.'")

A second, rote statement of like vintage:

Now I lay me down to sleep,
I pray the Lord my soul to keep;
And if I die before I wake,
I pray the Lord my soul to take.

No one discussed with me that this prayer statement might portray the Lord as theistic and directive. No one counseled me about deism and theism. This was just the way life was/is. And today with all my personal use of terms like: pinch of spirit and response-able; and theologians' use of terms like post-modernism and monophysitism, this childhood prayer is right in there as part of the exercise when we attempt our conceptualization of God.

It was a wondrous, proud day when the Lord's Prayer from Matthew's gospel was added to my list of the rote. Note that I learned it in the King James Version but I am very happy to say it now in later versions as:

"Our Father which art in Heaven, Hallowed be thy name. Thy kingdom come. Thy will be done in earth, as it is in Heaven. Give us this day our daily bread. And forgive us our debts, as we forgive our debtors. And lead us not into temptation, but deliver us from evil: For thine is the kingdom, and the power, and the glory, for ever. Amen."

This is an excellent prayer that condenses our life's "meaning and point" (see Richard Dawkins on atheism) to common sense if we ignore the theistic bent of some terms. The use of "Father" might be revisited in this day, the term Heaven bears scrutiny and I would suggest changing the two appearances of the word kingdom to kindom. Otherwise no morphing seems necessary.

Then came the super nova of rote, the wondrous day when I could state the Apostles Creed with no book. I still find this creed, the memory of Dr. Logan's very wet hand on my head, and the words confirmation and baptism stored together in my cerebral cortex where they have resided for 72 years.

Here is the creed in the form I learned it and as I still find it today in the Book of Confessions of the Presbyterian Church in the USA.

I believe in God the Father Almighty, Maker of heaven and earth,

And in Jesus Christ his only Son our Lord; who was conceived by the Holy Ghost, born of the Virgin Mary, suffered under Pontius Pilate, was crucified, dead, and buried; he descended into hell; the third day he rose again from the dead; he ascended into heaven, and sitteth at the right hand of God the Father Almighty; from thence he shall come to judge the quick and the dead.

I believe in the Holy Ghost, the holy catholic Church; the communion of saints; the forgiveness of sins; the resurrection of the body; and the life everlasting. Amen.

I can still recite the creed word for word –
but I don't.

TFTU 17. Transitioning from Inhibitions to Possibilities.

The simple joy that comes to us in the message, "God is Love," seems to disappear when the message is enhanced with embellishments and elaborate, theological conceptualizations of the nature of God. Why?

The simple joy of the child's song, "Jesus Loves Me," seems to disappear into a black hole of complexity when, at confirmation or any other time, we are presented with complicated creeds and religious mysticisms about Christ that we are told it will be an everlasting joy to believe. Why?

In several previous blogs I have offered the explanation that these dilemmas require correction within the necessity for the church to morph so that it can survive. If I were alone in discerning these "whys?" as problems, I would lay down my pen, unplug my computer, tuck my belief system under my pillow and sleep out my remaining days.

However, I find peers within the church, peers who have left the church and peers who refuse to join the church - who share my concerns. It takes the joy out of our beliefs when the climate of cultures inhibits us from breathing the atmosphere of possibilities. When the institution, which claims to be the body of the Christ who loves us, weighs us down with creeds and mysticisms that confine our minds and spirits to a box that shrinks them - this is a major, perhaps the ultimate, inhibition.

I shall not structure a long litany of inhibitions. We all can make our individual lists. Here are a few I've come across.

The Bible is inerrant. (Is it? Check out the Creation and innumerable Old Testament stories.) The Bible is the Word of God (who, per Biblical accounts, acted horribly at times, and should have been embarrassed to pass on such behavior as - The Word). This Unpleasant Yahweh was morphed into the controversial Trinity in the early centuries of the church. The conception of Jesus, counter to all natural, biogenic law, was attributed to the **Holy Spirit**. It is stated that **Comprehensible God as a Father** later manipulated **Mary's Son Jesus** into and through suffering, dying, being buried, descending into hell, being resurrected, ascending into heaven as homoousious (Christ per the bishops at Nicea 325 A.D.) joining and sitting next to homoousious (God per Nicea) and finally is to come back to save some humans and damn others. The Holy Ghost we are to believe in directs us to a belief in the holy inhibiting church; the communion of inhibited saints; the forgiveness of sins we should have avoided; and the resurrection of worn-out bodies we are to make do with in an everlasting life.

I have stated previously that too often we proclaim faith while practicing manipulation. This observation can be phrased in another manner: Too often the church proclaims joy for all while practicing inhibition.

Through the years I have gradually come to the realization the church is proclaiming joy while stifling my pinch of spirit with inhibitions and; if I don't transition from those inhibitions to the Atmosphere of Possibilities, I will smother. This is what I mean when I say that I must transition from inhibitions to possibilities to morph my belief system.

Nor can we forget that our purpose is to morph the church, not destroy it. We must be prepared for the internal guilt that comes from breaking our traditions and mind sets, even those we have come to recognize as harmful. We must be prepared for the external guilt that our culture will heap upon us, even as that culture has grave doubts of its own sanctimonious positions and practices.

Coming up in the next blog – The fear, worry and guilt of transitioning.

TFTU 18 What Did Pogo Mean?

This morning as I was in the Nautilus Exercise Room trying to coax the Elliptical Training Machine to register 1.7 miles in 16 minutes and burn up 150 calories, I looked at the blank screen of the turned off TV and thought of a previous blog. The one in which I imagined that the words of Pogo appeared on my blank computer screen as, "We have met the enemy and he is us."

I just now fed the word Pogo into my computer's, files' search engine and I find that Pogo's quote appeared in my blog of Monday, April 28, 2008 titled: "Enemies and Ghosts." I thought to myself, "What did Pogo mean?" It occurs to me that the biggest enemy we may meet as we attempt to morph the church will be our feelings of guilt. "We have met the enemy and he is us."

However we must not forget that our purpose is to morph the church, not destroy it. We must be prepared for the internal guilt that comes from breaking our traditions and mind sets, even those we have come to recognize as inhibitive. We must be prepared for the external guilt that our culture will heap upon us, even as that culture has grave doubts of its own sanctimonious positions and practices.

Just as there is a Holy Trinity designed by the early church to hold supportive sway over its adherents, there is an unholy triumvirate we design in our own minds which debilitates us. This is the trio of fear, worry and guilt.

Fear – Fear does pay dividends. They are worry.

Worry -- "Worry is a thin stream of fear trickling through the mind. If encouraged, it cuts a channel into which all other thoughts are drained." ~ Arthur Somers Roche

Guilt – "We have met the enemy and he is us." Pogo (My interpretation – our own worst enemy is us, debilitated by guilt.)

A little guilt and some inhibition, like a tonic, will give health to my conscience and steady my course. Excessive guilt and inhibition, like too much tonic, which is toxic, will debilitate my conscience and force my thoughts into the deep channel of fear.

If we will take the trusting leap into the Atmosphere of Possibilities, we can use those famous words from Franklin D. Roosevelt, "The only thing we have to fear is fear itself."

TFTU 19. Possibilities

Here again I credit Holmes Rolston III from whose: "Genes, Genesis and God, Their Origins in Natural and Human History" (p.367), I quoted earlier:

"The divine spirit is the giver of life, pervasively present over the millennia. God is the atmosphere of possibilities, the metaphysical environment, in, with, and under first the natural and later also the cultural environment, luring the Earthen histories upslope."

I find this modern statement of the nature of God plus the ageless Biblical statement, "God is Love," adequate to lure me to response-ableness.

God is Love requires no explanation.

What is the atmosphere of possibilities?

I have based my thinking beyond the box on the premise that the God of the Universe is incomprehensible even though humankind perpetuates boxes of ABCs and books of verses that try to render God comprehensible within humanly developed and proscribed parameters e.g. specific religions, specific times, specific cultures, specific scriptures, specific rituals, etc.

Earlier I have presented the personal belief statement that sustains me in this new atmosphere beyond the box. Here it is again:

"I believe that the Incomprehensible God of the Universe is an Atmosphere of Possibilities within which the human can be a response-able steward to and for the Incomprehensible God – and responsible to and with all of humanity, including self."

In the past many have chosen to break with the church as a part of attempting to escape its inhibitions:
- denying the church as an authentic agent of God.
- rejecting God along with rejecting the church.
- desisting from participation in organized religion.
- forming new churches with nebulous missions.
- developing a reclusive relationship with "their" God.
- etc.

Here I would repeat a paragraph from TFTU #18. What Did Pogo Mean?

However we must not forget that our purpose is to morph the church, not destroy it. We must be prepared for the internal guilt that comes from breaking our traditions and mind sets, even those we have come to recognize as inhibitive. We must be prepared for the external guilt that our culture will heap upon us, even as that culture has grave doubts of its own sanctimonious positions.

If we are to morph the church we must first develop a belief that includes our being response-able to God and responsible to all of humanity - stated in our own words.

As I strive to think beyond the box the church continues to endorse, I will continue to support this church and denomination in its compassionate works and, in turn, welcome its support within a communion of fellowship.

I will resist inhibiting manipulations within the Christian Faith. I will present my beliefs as something to be considered, not as truths that must be accepted. I will courageously present my belief system while encouraging others to present theirs. I will honor the healthy, non-harmful beliefs of others. I will listen to understand. I will speak to affirm.

I will encourage my peers within and without the church to hold those beliefs that give them the joy of being response-able to Incomprehensible God and responsible to comprehensible humanity.

Although God is incomprehensible in total, when our leap of faith takes us into the Atmosphere of Possibilities a trust develops within us that makes many things possible. When I transition from inhibitions to possibilities my response-ableness broadens. When **we** transition from inhibitions to possibilities our relationships broaden. When **the church** transitions from inhibitions to possibilities its stewardship within the total Kindom will broaden... **and the church will survive.**

Blessed Are the Uninhibited for They Shall Recognize the Atmosphere of Possibilities.

TFTU 20. And Now – In Conclusion

Blessed Are the Uninhibited for They Shall Recognize the Atmosphere of Possibilities.

I have discovered, as I think beyond the box, that the ABCs of the box (doctrines, tenets, rituals, symbols and our various religious conceptualizations of comprehensible God) pale alongside our becoming response-able stewards to/for the Incomprehensible God of the Universe.

Within the Atmosphere of Possibilities it is not our mission to convert humanity to specific religions. It is our mission to convert (morph) ourselves to being response-able to the Incomprehensible God of the Universe and responsible to/with all of humanity within the *Kindom* of God.

In an April 21, 2008 blog titled, "Why Morphing Is Difficult," one of my most beneficial questioners asked me:

"a. Exactly what is it that you advocate morphing?
b. Is it the Presbyterian Church in the USA?

c. Is it the Christian Church in the World?

d. Is it the All in All of human religion?"

Here were my answers in April, 2008:

a. Currently it is my personal belief system. (Timeline = my lifetime)

b. Eventually yes, the Presbyterian Church in the USA. (Timeline unknown)

c. Eventually yes, the Christian Church in the World. (Timeline unknown)

d. Eventually yes, the All in All of Human Religion. (Timeline Infinity)

And now...with 2008 morphing into 2009, I find that my answers have changed as I understand more clearly what it is to think beyond the box. Thinking beyond the box is not like the abrupt metamorphosis of a caterpillar into a butterfly. It is more the evolutionary morphing of innocent errancies (faulty conceptualizations) into functional possibilities. Here I take the reader back to the January 23, 2007 blog, "God Is The Atmosphere of Possibilities." and quote from "Genes, Genesis and God, Their Origins in Natural and Human History" by Holmes Rolston, III.

"The divine spirit is the giver of life, pervasively present over the millennia. God is the atmosphere of possibilities, the metaphysical environment, in, with, and under first the natural and later also the cultural environment, luring the Earthen histories upslope."

Rolston does not say that the divine spirit is a directive (theistic) God **pulling** or **pushing** Earthen histories upslope. He says that God is the atmosphere of possibilities **luring** the Earthen histories (and this of course includes *humankind*) upslope. My thinking beyond the box releases me from the comprehensible, directing God of the Bible verse within the climate of cultures to the Incomprehensible, Luring God of the Universe - within the Atmosphere of Possibilities.

As I have come to this realization my answers must change.

Question a. was:

"Exactly what is it that you advocate morphing?"

I ventured that it was my belief system and morphing it would consume my lifetime. I now hope that this is not true. I find myself adequately fulfilled at this point in my evolutionary morphing so that I am ready to float as a butterfly rather than struggle as an inhibited caterpillar.

As I have come to think further beyond the box, my conceptualization of religion has tilted toward its functionality rather than its form. Within all evolutionary processes the seminal, driving law is that form follows function.

The form of a fin evolved for the function of swimming must change to the form of a wing for flying or to a limb for climbing.

This is why I could introduce this concluding blog with the conviction that it is not our mission to convert humanity to specific religions (forms) – it is our mission to convert (morph) ourselves to becoming responsible to/with all of humanity within the Kindom of God (function).

Questions b, c and d in the listing of April 21, 2008 deal with present and future forms of religions and religious institutions. When I answered the questions in April, 2008 I spoke from the tradition of forms. As I have come to realize how different the Atmosphere of Possibilities is from the climate of cultures I am aware that I have no idea what "form" religion will take when humans, response-able to the Incomprehensible God of the Universe, function responsibly for/with fellow humans in the Kindom of God.

The Wednesday, June 06, 2007 blog was:

"Incomprehensible or Doctrinal?" In that blog I touched on the tremendous gap which exists when we conceptualize God as comprehensible through human generated doctrines as contrasted with the awe which we should feel when we try to conceptualize the Incomprehensible God of the Universe.

In his book, "The Pale Blue Dot" Carl Sagan summarizes this vital concept much more succinctly:

"A religion, old or new, that stressed the magnificence of the Universe as revealed by modern science might be able to draw forth reserves of reverence and awe hardly tapped by conventional faiths. Sooner or later such a religion will emerge."

I have no idea what the form of that religion will be. I do know what its function will be – to demonstrate that the Incomprehensible God of the Universe is that Love within the Atmosphere of Possibilities luring Earthen histories upslope.

Epilogue

It is when we think beyond the box in which we store our proofs of the comprehensible God that we realize that God is Incomprehensible.

It is when we realize that God is Incomprehensible that we can recognize God as the Atmosphere of Possibilities.

Although at times the Christian Faith appears to compress God into -- Our God, The Word, Logos, God of the Bible, Homoousios, Father, Son, Holy Spirit -- the church, to its credit, does not intentionally confine God in the box. It confines only those items that the church utilizes to prove the comprehensible nature of God. Even the ancient Israelites, as they structured the Ark of the Covenant with its intricate box and two cherubim, did not confine God to the box, but proclaimed that God hovered as spirit between the two cherubim -- above the box.

This series of blogs started with a blog posted on May 27, 2005, titled – "It's Beyond Me." Within the course of this 3+ years' series of blogs I have been in contact with many who fear for the future of the church. I have met but a miniscule number of peers who deny totally that the church is at risk of dying. My early exposure to a formal recognition of this potential death was Bishop John Shelby Spong's book titled, "Why Christianity Must Change Or Die."

For some this phrase has gradually changed to – "The church must change or die." Somewhere along the way within this blog series I took the liberty of softening the phrase to – "The church must morph to survive." (Blog of Thursday, November 29, 2007, "More on Cause")

As I thought of the church morphing it was apparent that the only way the church could morph was for its members to morph – and this meant – guess who?

What was I to morph?

My religion?

Dictionaries and encyclopedias define religion as:

a particular system of faith and worship.

I do not perceive morphing religion to be within my scope. One caveat however: If I seek true learning (about) religion (Holmes Rolston III) see Blog TFB 3. "Designing the Course," I am required to stretch beyond asking, "What is true about our religion," to asking, "whether our religion is true."

Morph my belief system?

Encyclopedias define a belief system as: the system on which beliefs are based. For example a religious belief system is based on faith and dogma whereas a scientific belief system is based on observation and reason. My faith happens when my pinch of spirit is response-able to the Incomprehensible God, the Atmosphere of Possibilities. Faith will change as Possibilities change.

Although some dogmas may not change, so long as I remain uninhibited I can choose that dogma which I trust most.

Therefore, yes, I can morph my belief system.

Needing to morph my belief system was not a surprise to me. I'd been at it for years. This blog series, now presented as a book, describes that process in abundant detail. The process can be summarized in my belief statement that has evolved:

"I believe that the Incomprehensible God of the Universe is an Atmosphere of Possibilities within which the human can be a response-able steward to and for the Incomprehensible God – and responsible to and with all of humanity, including self."

Here follows what I said about this statement of belief in my November 17, 2008 Blog:

"This is not intended to be a theological statement. It is my *conceptualization* of being response-able to God. It is not a *comprehension* of what we must believe to be saved - **someday**. It is my very own conceptualization for a joyous survival in an atmosphere of possibilities, that gets me by - **in these days** - to whatever follows."

These statements work for me. That is no proof that they will work for you. Hence you will probably prefer to design your own.

Now, how about the statement – "The church must morph to survive." The reader will note that the blog series did not outline an elaborate plan on that subject. Morphing is an evolutionary process for individual church members and a **form** (a morphed church or something else?) will evolve in response to the **functioning** of these morphed individuals. (As in all evolutionary processes the law that "form follows function" applies. This is true of all things inorganic and organic; physical and metaphysical.)

Some hold the prohibitive caveat that the church was designed by the actions of a theistic, directive God and thus its form cannot be morphed by the functionality of morphed adherents. If this is true why would the directive God now permit the church to die?

No! - Form follows function is a law within the Atmosphere of Possibilities that cannot be inhibited by adherents or institutions (churches).

Here I would repeat the closing paragraph of Blog TFTU #19. "Possibilities:"

"Although God is incomprehensible in total, when our leap of faith takes us into the Atmosphere of Possibilities a trust develops within us that makes many things possible. When **I** transition from inhibitions to possibilities my response-ableness broadens. When **we** transition from inhibitions to possibilities our relationships broaden. When **the church** transitions from inhibition to possibilities its stewardship within the total Kindom will broaden ... **and the church will survive."**

We cannot predict the form but that form will survive;
because --

Blessed is the church that morphs from suffocation in a climate of cultures to survival within the Atmosphere of Possibilities.

Ω

Glossary

ABCs in – "The box to be thought beyond:"
A. Factious Fundamentals and Doctrines.
B. Embellished Stories and Myths.
C. Outmoded Knowledge and Cultures.
ableness – a coined noun to express the state of being;
e.g. response-able, response-ableness. See response-able.
agnostic – noun - a person who believes that nothing is known or
can be known of the existence or nature of God or anything beyond
material phenomena; a person who claims neither faith nor disbelief
in God.
atheism – noun – the theory or belief that God does not exist.
atheist – noun – one who subscribes to the theory of atheism.
Atmosphere of Possibilities – See Incomprehensible God.
belief system – the conceptualized system on which beliefs are
based. For example a religious belief system is based on faith and
dogma whereas a scientific belief system is based on observation and
reason.
churchology – a coined noun to set forth the study of
the nature and functions of churches.
churchological – a coined adjective to describe studies
pertaining to the church in its many forms.
co-creators - a term this author first heard used by Rev. Bill Peterson
as pastor of the Salem (IN) Presbyterian Church in about 1996. As

he used the term its context was that humans are co-creators of the future with God. I have broadened the context to state that humans are co-creators with each other and with God in the present and future within the Atmosphere of Possibilities.

Comprehensible God of the Bible Verse (the Climate of Cultures) - God as recorded in the writings of previous cultures. (See Incomprehensible God of the Universe, the Atmosphere of Possibilities).

created-image humans - Biblical language states that the human is created in the image of God. If we can avoid the anthropomorphic conceptualization of God looking like a human (physical) and grasp the conceptualization of the human portraying some of God's love (spiritual) this term has valid use.

deism – noun – belief in the existence of a supreme being, specifically a creator who does not intervene in the universe. The term is used chiefly as an intellectual movement in the 17th and 18th centuries that accepted the existence of a creator on the basis of reason but rejected belief in a supernatural deity who interacts with humankind. Compare with theism.

dogma – a principle or set of principles laid down by an authority as incontrovertibly true.

errant – deviating from the regular or proper course.

errancy – a coined noun to express the state of being errant. See innocent-errancy.

evangelism – the human sharing of God's love within all of humanity.

faith - The Nature of God is Love. The nature of the human is to be response-able to God. This is faith.

Gnostic – noun - an adherent of Gnosticism.

Gnosticism – noun - a prominent heretical movement of the 2nd Century Christian Church, partly of pre Christian origin, Gnostic doctrine taught that the world was created and ruled by a lesser divinity, the demiurge, and that Christ was an emissary of the remote supreme divine being - esoteric knowledge (gnosis) of whom enabled the redemption of the human spirit.

Incomprehensible God of the Universe (the Atmosphere of Possibilities) – that beyond comprehension that lures humanity upslope to its spiritual potential. (See Comprehensible God of the Bible Verse, the Climate of Cultures)

inerrant – free from error; incapable of error

innocent-errancy – a coined term to express the state of believing errant information innocently because it is the best explanation currently available. e.g. The world is flat (1491), the Biblical creation stories, the early concept that the Sun rotated around the Earth.

 Kindom of God – a coined term to describe the relationship of all humans as being kin within God rather than subjects of God as a king. (Origin unknown)

Kingdom of God – a term used in ancient times to describe Heaven and Earth as the domain of God in human geo-political terms. The term continues into the present age as a selective term for believers (those in the Kingdom) and non-believers (those outside the Kingdom).

over-comprehend – to claim a faith beyond normal, healthy response-ableness to God. eg. to claim a relationship with God stronger than that of other created-image humans.

pinch of spirit in the human – a term borrowed from Arnold Toynbee's concept of the connectional relationship between Creator God and created humans.

Quinitarian – a modern, coined supposition that God functions as Creator, Sustainer, Redeemer, Mediator and Savior. (See Trinitarian)

relationships – the most powerful ships afloat.

religion – the belief in and worship of a superhuman controlling power, esp, a personal God or gods.

- a particular system of faith or worship that connects the human to the superhuman.

response-able – the innate ability of every human to respond to God. A more powerful concept than being responsible to God as a vaguely defined quality.

revelation-deprived – if there are times, places and persons to whom God makes disproportionate revelations, this would infer that God's Grace is disproportionate. It would infer that all other times, places and peoples are revelation-deprived. If God is Love, if God is Grace, how can there be revelation-deprivation?

theism – noun – belief in the existence of a god or gods, esp. belief in one god as creator of the universe, intervening in it and sustaining a personal relation to "his"
Creatures. Compare with deism.

Trinitarian – an ancient doctrine that God exists in three forms: Father, Son and Holy Spirit.

uniquity – a noun coined from the adjective unique.
e.g. That which is a uniquity, pl. uniquities.

worship – God is love within all of the universe and within all of humanity. Worship is humanity beseeching God to share that love so it can be used in respect for the totality of the universe and humanity.

Is My Belief System Really Mine?

In a previous book I made the claim that my belief system was, "A Belief System From The General Store," part of the culture in which I grew up.

Through many years I accepted the church's teachings that my beliefs were to come from the ABCs within a box describing the Comprehensible God of the Bible Verse, the Climate of Cultures.

Now a new persuasion from beyond the box is encouraging me to be response-able to the Incomprehensible God of the Universe, the Atmosphere of Possibilities wherein I am to be responsible to all of humanity, including myself.

Hence, in this book I declare, "A Belief System From Beyond The Box."

Is a belief system really mine if it derives from a climate of previous cultures and fails to recognize the atmosphere of possibilities surrounding us?

Can the human comprehend God or does the human conceptualize God? Can cultures comprehend God or do cultures conceptualize God?

As my belief system has become more and more my own, beyond the rote ABCs, my inhibitions (internal guilt) and my fears (external peer pressures) have morphed away from the coercions existing when I thought I comprehended God as the Comprehensible God of the Bible Verse, the Climate of Cultures.

Now I am coming to recognize God as the Incomprehensible God of the Universe, the Atmosphere of Possibilities.

Will our personal, post-morphing beliefs – from beyond the box – give the church the opportunity to morph and survive?

I believe they will when we shift from conceptualizing God as a Climate of Cultures to recognizing God as an Atmosphere of Possibilities.

Suggested Readings:

The God Delusion
   Houghton-Miflin-Harcourt, Richard Dawkins

The Phenomenon of Man
   Harper and Row, N.Y. Teilhard de Chardin

The Greatest Thing in the World
   (Collins) Great Britain, Henry Drummond

Abraham: A Journey to the Heart of Three Faiths
   Perennial, Bruce Feiler

If Grace Is True
   Harper San Francisco, Phillip Gulley and James Mulholland

I Have a Dream
   Grosset & Dunlap, Martin Luther King, Jr.

Man's Search for Himself
   W. W. Norton and Co. Rollo May

The Suicidal Church

Pluto Press Australia, Caroline Miley

Beyond Belief – the Secret Gospel of Thomas
Vintage Books, Elaine Pagels

Your God is Too Small
Simon Shuster, New York, J. B. Phillips

Mark Twain's Religion
Mercer University Press, William E. Phipps

Genes, Genesis, and God
Cambridge Univ. Press, Holmes Rolston, III

Religious Inquiry
Philosophical Library, Holmes Rolston, III

Pale Blue Dot
Random House, Carl Sagan

Why Christianity Must Change or Die
Harper San Francisco, John Shelby Spong

A New Earth
A Plume Book, Eckhart Tolle

A Study of History
Oxford Univ. Press, N.Y. Arnold J. Toynbee

About the Author

How does an author tell a readership enough about himself/ herself that readers acknowledge the writer as authentic? How does the biography stop short of an appearance of boasting? How can one fulfill both of these requirements?

I believe that I am an authentic church member adequately engaged in the mission of my particular denomination of the Christian Faith. I have been an elder in my local church for more than 60 years, serving my share of the duties vital to its continued existence. I have participated in the next higher judicatory, presbytery, as a frequent committee member, on administrative commissions, as moderator and as a delegate to multiple General Assemblies.

We need to feel authentic. I do feel authentic. But being authentic is not the issue at hand. One could be an authentic member of the inauthentic Flat Earth Society. The issue at hand is this:

Are the beliefs in the box we have been handed by past cultures relevant to the times in which we live?

Are the concepts in this book relevant to the morphing and survival of the Christian church? Here I repeat some material from the May 30, 2008 blog:

"Friday, May 30, 2008

It's Beyond the Box

"As I go back to the first blog that I released into cyberspace, I discover that the date was May 27, 2005 and the title was, 'It's Beyond Me.'

"As I scan forward through the Archives of all the postings to the present, I find that two major themes have developed synergistically:

1. That segment of the formal religious establishment described loosely by the term church, is under stress. The extreme nature of this stress is demonstrated by the current, often-quoted, fearsome phrase – 'The Church must change or it will die.'

2. The most frequently offered response to this dilemma is the admonition, 'We must think beyond the box.'

"Pragmatism indicates that: 'The Church must change or it will die,' phrase is hopelessly destructive. Might this prediction be more approachable if rephrased as? 'The Church must morph, then survive.'

"Survival indicates that: It is essential that we determine what it is in the box that we must think beyond."

In this series of blogs, and the resultant book, I have tried to discover what is in the box we must think beyond that should be changed so that our belief systems can morph, thus equipping the church to morph to survival.

It is my conclusion that my past conceptualizations of God, my core beliefs, have been formed by inhibiting Climates of Cultures, deposited in the box over the ages in a futile attempt to make God comprehensible. It is my emerging discovery that when we think beyond the box we recognize the Atmosphere of Possibilities, the Incomprehensible God of the Universe.

Though our core beliefs may differ we should be encouraged, and encourage our peers, to hold beliefs that give us the joy of being response-able to Incomprehensible God, the Atmosphere of Possibilities, and responsible to/with comprehensible humanity.

Printed in the United States
144900LV00003B/8/P

9 781438 967882